Contents

The Occulted Suburb

Peter Lang

Long considered kitschy, consumerist, and self-serving, the suburb in America has been a target for radical reconstruction. Yet given that the suburban quilt reaches across entire sections of this country, with even historic villages fading into its fabric, planners' more immediate concerns are to divine its ways and deconstruct its trends. The early leaders of suburban archaeology and sociology, from Lewis Mumford to Herbert Marcuse, did not fully anticipate just how popular the American fixation with the single-family home and its winding driveway would become. Successive generations of critics have continued to detail the detrimental conditions of suburbia on communities and the environment, but few have been able to convincingly explore the suburb's enormous appeal outside the standard framework predicated on urban flight.

In truth, suburbia and suburban culture hardly deserve such mistreatment. The success of the American suburbs, like that of a film panned by the critics but a hit with the public, is best measured by the size of its audience. The American city—the emphatic city, the city of lore, and the city of dreams—no longer will command a preeminent role in the coming century. All roads lead, by now, through suburbia. Bread and circuses are now available at McDonald's and on Howard Stern's radio show. Incontestably, the pull of the suburb is a force with which to be reckoned.

Outside the United States the phenomenon of territorial marginalization solicits far more troubling responses.[1] The suburb in South America or in Europe is similarly territorial and just as forcefully expansive as its American counterpart, but does not function as a receptacle for middle-class values. These are lands on the margin: the neglected front lines of the emerging classes, the ramshackle gardens of primordial villages, or the vertiginous playgrounds for a new generation in power. These peripheries are the heirs to Henry Miller's Clichy. In Europe, where urban regional expansion was historically state administered, the peripheries are viewed as potentially explosive grounds for social unrest. State planning in these areas are often masked efforts in social engineering. The truly innovative contributions emerging from these outcast communities have not yet been sufficiently understood by the dominant society.

Though these vast areas on the outskirts of ancient city centers may not be choice sites like the American suburbs, they are the areas with growing populations and energetic signs of new cultural mixes. If you want to know what is really happening in Rome, go out to the Corviale, the kilometer-long social housing project in the southern part of the city.[2]

Suburban or marginal regions across the globe reflect the latest evolving trends in contemporary culture. Beneath a veil of stereotyped uniformity lurk insomniacs and amnesiacs, plagued by fear or driven to invention. Poetry and violence, romance and pornography, and organic gardens and toxic waste are all nestled into the naturalistic settings of the suburbs. Modernity was never further than just around the corner.

What then is the precise nature of the rising suburban culture. How can it be defined outside the tired dialectic between town and country? What are the rituals and customs, the monuments and follies, the morals and fantasies of contemporary suburbs?

To study the synthetic relationship between environment and society that is the suburb is to enter the region of suburban discipline. To reach beyond the superficial layers of readings that have for so long marked the contours of this subject, a diverse group of critics, historians, and first-hand observers have been invited to reflect on the suburb in the States and

THE OCCULTED SUBURB

abroad. I have no pretension that the work collected here represents in any way a complete discussion on the structures and mores of the contemporary periphery. Rather, I am pleased to offer what I consider a small but important contribution to the suburban polemic: the occulted suburb.

When I recently revisited the omnipresent suburb I was struck by how far off the mark my picture of the place really was. Many of the local customs, like hanging out at the 7-Eleven or going to the mall, continue to be part of coming-of-age rituals. But other rites, like gathering with other immigrant laborers in the early mornings or late afternoons, are subtle examples of a less familiar culture. No longer is the contemporary suburb the stuff of television reruns. Yet television's diaphanous images have spread a shroud on the American collective conscious. We think we know what happens in the suburbs, but we are missing many sides to the story.

The ungraspable nature of this subject seems only to deflect the true weight of suburban culture. Suburbia continues to remain occulted by the multiple dimensions of its geography and the extreme provinciality of its past. Yet the presence of a living culture is a *sine qua non* of history. There is no lock-step path to the hearts and minds of the suburbanite. In the region that is occupied by the suburb, society has achieved its consensus. Somewhere in the spatial and temporal world of suburbia there exist the reasons for its tremendous gut appeal.

1. Roger Silverstone, ed., *Visions of Suburbia* (New York: Routledge, 1997) restricts its focus to English, North American, and Australian suburbs. I have used a broader definition of suburbia in *Suburban Discipline* in order to probe what is increasingly becoming a global phenomenon across marginal territories.
2. Romans refer to the Corviale as the "Bronx." The project was designed by the architect Mario Fiorentino in 1972 and completed in 1975, and houses 9000 inhabitants.

Peter Lang is an architect and historian. He has recently completed a year as a Fulbright Fellow in modern history in Rome, Italy.

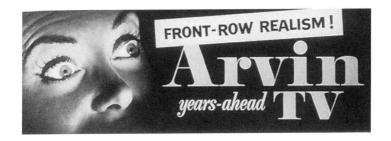

Adorably unself-conscious, this billboard relates the way drivers see to the fixations of a public addicted to a new mass medium that makes it a willing accomplice in its own visual bondage. All that looking—drivers gawking, ad characters staring, TV sets beaming—makes for a visual stew that indicates the era's love of the panoply of new and old ways of seeing.

Visual Browsing: Auto-flâneurs and Roadside Ads in the 1950s

Kathleen Hulser

The suburbs in America were midwifed at Henry Ford's Red River plant. By the 1950s, car culture had so grafted itself onto everyday life that many suburbanites had become auto-centaurs, joined to their vehicles at the waist. While their torsos were draped over steering wheels, their eyes surveyed the world through the windshield. And what life could be glimpsed through that scrim? A world of billboard advertisements, neon signs, body and chrome shops, roadside fast-food restaurants, and shopping plazas. In essence, the distracted driving mode of inattentive looking was bolstered by a man-made environment of glitz, desire, and consumer paraphernalia meant for desultory, fleeting sampling.

Thus, the link between the heavy diet of billboard advertising consumed through the windshield and the way a driver saw in the 1950s fostered a kind of perception I call that of the "auto-flâneur." This notion connects a typically modern mode of transit with an evolving mode of perception. The concept "auto-flâneur" is inspired by Charles Baudelaire, Georg Simmel, and Walter Benjamin, who have suggested how capitalism, urbanity, and modernity affect sensory experience. In this case, however, the billboard landscape of suburbia illuminates the syndrome.[1]

Auto-flâneur's wheeled mobility refers mostly to orbiting known environs, not to the determined looking of the tourist in a new place. The auto-flâneur operates in a timeless present of being *en route*, rather than hastening to a destination. Auto-flânerie consists of a gaze that any generation or gender might experience when driving. However, the most striking illustration of that mode of perception is among those consummate time wasters: teenagers, hotrodders, crypto-delinquents, and young singles. In the eye of the auto-flâneur, the familiar roadside is a movielike montage of discrete elements sequenced in a familiar way, even as billboards changed their ads and roadside chains and strip malls multiplied. Indeed, during the 1960s 40,000 hopefuls a year poured their savings into opening franchises, many oriented to suburban traffic, where highway locations were cheap.

The public landscape of 1950s and 1960s suburbia centered on the road, which business saw as a moving conveyor belt of potential consumers. While the suburb rejected the business face of the city, it offered a similar buffet of consumer culture, here packaged as part of leisure and pleasure, far from work. Visual sampling of the buffet began with the driver's unconscious perusal of roadside architecture and signage.

Much of the visual experience of driving is implicit in the billboard industry's approach to imprinting icons on the public mind. Since the 1920s, billboard creators had been enlarging the image and shrinking the text, thereby making the ads less about reading and more about momentary subconscious impacts. Industry handbooks advised using not more than seven words, creating strong profiles and silhouettes, and reducing detail in favor of huge swathes of paint.[2] The horsepower behemoths produced by 1950s Detroit made brevity even more crucial, as rising car speeds turned glances into gulps.

For instance, a mid-1950s Pepsi ad from the Pacific Outdoor Advertising Company featured a nearly fifty-foot-long woman in pedal pushers, whose red blouse covered yards of the painted bulletin. Shown reclining on one hip like some Gidget Olympia, she caressed her kitty as two monumental Pepsi bottles sprouted behind her legs. Although the visual syntax was modern, the giant female figure in the landscape also attempted to capture the response that anthropomorphic geographic forms used to have on traditional cultures. As distant twin hills had been called the "mother range," such modern commercial depictions implied a similar earth/mother/fertility connection. Individually painted works with cut-out edges that made the horizon function as part of the image could be truly gargantuan, compared to the standard thirty-six-foot-long display. Industry experts calculated that the consumer glance lasted about six seconds at highway speeds. With this in mind, billboard designers cooperated with graphic designers to infiltrate public memory with an unconscious vocabulary of logo imagery that became the keynote of roadside chains, television advertising, and billboard legibility.

What was it about driving that made people see differently? Through the frame of the windshield, structures of perception work with the color and contrasts of the image, the distance of objects from the body, and the pace of the body in motion. Spectatorship of the road trained drivers in a mode of seeing that allowed a visual command of a wide range of objects without actually being in a physical relationship to them. It both fed curiosity and fostered detachment. Viewing the passing scene from behind a wheel integrated roadside elements into a fleeting but satisfying glance that had more to do with submerging oneself in an experience than surveying a lovely prospect.

Sometimes advertisers even acknowledged this peculiar dialectic of the gaze. A bug-eyed woman popping from a TV set itself meets the gaze of the driver in a billboard advertisement for Arvin TV. The woman's stunned and mesmerized aura echoes a similar state in the intended audience. It was as though watching TV could put viewers in a trance equivalent to that of the voyeuristic auto-flâneur transfixed by the roadside show.

Roads connected work life and private life in new patterns in suburbia. Roads helped workers escape to "residential" areas, yet also pried open their wallets to dispense those wages on lifestyle related goods acquired in roadside emporia. The classic bedroom suburbs of the 1950s forced the employed to drive to their jobs, usually in the city. Their commutes in snarling lanes of traffic could hardly be characterized as a prime pleasure of suburbia. Yet, the relationship to the car in advertising, in the popular imagination, and in values still seemed largely euphoric in those days. The idea of commuting in a personally chosen and appointed shell, a mobile unit of autonomy, seemed to compensate for the rigors of rush-hour road time. Detroit advertising tirelessly broadcast this image of the car as icon of freedom and personality, leaving out the traffic, boredom, and wasted time. In one 1955 billboard, a Ford Fairlane V-8 leaps off the board with its fender extended off the sign. Implying that the sky itself is the "fair lane," the simple image evokes the airborne aspirations of 1950s styling.

How did the other gender fit into this paradigm of the good life? One in ten suburban women worked for pay, far fewer than the one in four women in the city. Suburbanites tended to be younger—thirty-one on average in 1950—and to have more children than city dwellers.[3] But automobility for women in the suburbs tended to be less than that for men—a disadvantage not bestowed by gender in the city with its public transit systems. As scathingly noted in Betty Friedan's 1963 *The Feminine Mystique*, the suburb without a car often constituted a mental Siberia.[4] One appliance ad on 1955 billboards unconsciously imaged the problem: the housewife whizzing around her living room with a Lewyt vacuum was amputated at the waist, since her role demanded of her only the task-oriented hands and legs. Yet, the 1950s dress code dictated that this woman/appliance wear a kicky skirt and high heels, as though she were about to skip out to a record hop.

Carlessness was bad enough for homemakers, but the stifling gender roles of the period often made owning wheels a scant improvement. For the growing number of women that made Detroit smile by buying second cars, the life of "shuttle-mom," chauffeuring offspring to sports, music lessons, and shopping malls, had as little appeal as staying home. A woman's car tended to function as an appliance that made her duties as chauffeur and shopper possible, rather than as a vehicle of imagination, power, and freedom, as implied in ads aimed at men. Yet families with two or more cars went from seven percent of the population in 1950 to twenty-seven percent by 1969.

Reality might easily contradict the grossly materialist pitch of a 1956 Ford billboard showing a red wagon and two-tone convertible snuggling under a carport, with the tag line "4 bedrooms, 3 baths . . . 2 Fords." Colored like a cardinal perched next to a Baltimore oriole, the wagon and "personal luxury vehicle" said

The vacuum-head image of this woman/appliance offers the flip side of the male auto-centaur joined to his car at the waist. For her, a vacuum replaces the vestigial head no longer needed for a suburban woman, whereas for him, the amputation at waist works because the car itself is all the legs and sex organs a modern man really needs.

The woodcut-derived image of the Grim Reaper reminds drivers that modernity and tradition may mix violently at the roadside. Taken from a campaign posted in the Bible Belt, the scene contrasts with the usual cheery pitches of 1950s billboards.

as much with color as with form. The utilitarian wagon for shuttle-mom wore a jaunty crimson coat. But for the real peacock in the family, the Thunderbird convertible in yellow with black and chrome trim sang a seductive song of debonair cruising.

This polarized view of the genders' auto pleasures reflects a common stereotype of the time. Both suburbanites and the media tended to depict suburbs as the place of family, children, time after work, consumption, and leisure, as opposed to the hard-headed, wage-earning, business-driven, and political bustle of the city.[5] But the seeming opposition of the enhanced domesticity of the suburb and the out-of-home free-wheeling of car culture actually forms a dependent duo. Living in the 'burbs meant putting ever more people on wheels. Selling Americans massive quantities of new cars inevitably created an endless supply of used cars, often affordable to the young or those unworthy of credit. If owning a car was part and parcel of owning a house in the suburbs, the car also provided personal space outside the hyper-coded family space of the home. Wheels could just as well speed your flight from the family as hasten you home. And even the tendency in the suburbs to eliminate sidewalks and have the garage at front connect directly to the road emphasized the notion that the home was another stop at a drive-in, a temporary destination in a life conceptualized as the car.

Of course, not all bought into the suburban ideal. Essayist Philip Wylie called drivers "suckers for the illusion that movement connoted advancement," and went on to howl in his best-selling jeremiad against maternal dominance and consumer society:

> The American moral rout is best of all exemplified by the automobile and what business did with it. . . . Man drove. He drove to the corner for cigarettes. He drove to the club. He drove to the office. He drove around for the hell of it . . . "to get away from himself." . . . He rode in his sheet-iron womb, carried by the matriarchy, lulled with the wayside show which swirled past as analgesically and as blindingly as amniotic fluid.[6]

The Washington road lobby, a cabal of auto industrialists, oil barons, and highway engineers, contributed to the official versions of the pro-driving and pro-car good life. For example, a film of the 1950s, produced by the National Highway Users Association (Detroit's federal lobbying arm), was titled "Mobility: The Fifth Freedom" and aimed to stimulate taxpayer demand for roads as part of their "natural right" to drive on good highways.[7] United States Census Bureau numbers shows this vision triumphant. New Deal employment projects had greatly increased road miles during the Depression, but the 1956 Defense Highways Act funded an additional 41,000 miles of interstate. Car registrations bolted upwards from 49 million in 1950 to 108 million by 1960. Families spent between eleven and fourteen percent of their personal income on cars, gas, and oil during the first twenty postwar years.

The car supplied both transportation to suburbia and an escape from its domestic disciplinary mode of work, home, and family. Consumption themes dominated the landscape at the same time as a teen culture of hot rods and strenuous "cool" denied those values. These two, often warring, categories of sub-urban drivers were both addressed by the advertising landscape aimed at the bulging middle class. If moms and pops depend-ably bought consumer durables, their offspring seemed to revel in capitalism's consumable and ephemeral pleasures: movies, records, cigarettes, beer, gas, and thick shakes.

Somehow wise before their years, these teens with attitude, or "rebels without a cause," as the movies called them, sensed a visible contradiction between the cheery world of roadside abun-dance and the mortgage bondage of their suburban dads, pinned to their identities as tax-payers, even as they dreamed of racing Corvettes across a salt flat. These teen aesthetics bumped up against the hygienic landscapes idolized by their elders. Why move from "dirty cities" to "clean suburbs" if roadside develop-ment was allowed to trash the area as fast as the highways were built? Reformers had been strategizing to regulate billboards for decades, and in 1954 the Supreme Court decided a test case. Favoring the beautifiers, Justice William O. Douglas wrote that aesthetic values formed a proper part of the government respon-sibility for "public welfare."

The concept of public welfare is broad and inclusive.... The values it represents are spiritual as well as physical, aesthetic as well as monetary. It is within the power of the legislature to determine that the community should be beautiful as well as healthy, spacious as well as clean, well-balanced as well as carefully patrolled.[8]

Douglas's Berman v. Parker opinion dealt with the constitutionality of an aesthetic public purpose in justifying urban renewal in Washington, DC to counteract "blight." But it supplied the legal foundation for making aesthetics part of the police powers that local laws could wield. Community activists eager to pass land-use laws to control local development hailed the decision.

Oddly enough, this advance in the community's right to determine the look of a place came just as attitudes towards what constituted a good-looking place were in turmoil. The lyric kitsch of the roadside and the auto-flâneur form of perception coincided with the rise of pop art in the art world. Pop art was an attitude born in the city, nourished in the art world, and kin to consumer culture. It offered a stance towards American advertising, roads, and architecture that could suit artist and worker alike. Phrased as radical populism, pop art called on liberal intellectuals to reevaluate the suburb and acknowledge that the car was a beloved feature of American life.

Whether blithely serving the billboard industry or splashing around the joys of a new attitude, pop art threw a new light on advertising. Just as Marshall McLuhan had discussed all high and low arts—commercial illustration and TV and easel painting—as one communication system, advertising could be seen as integral to culture, rather than a commercial excretion. Maybe as TV ads saturated the public eye, the brevity of the billboard text began to seem a relief. Or, signaling the developing pace of commercialism, there could have been a premature nostalgia brewing for an old-fashioned ad form. Meanwhile artists seemed to breathe in popular culture as part of an ironic, camp attitude towards their own conflicting feelings. ("Popular culture is easy and fun, so it is a guilty pleasure, unworthy of the creative elite, but it has so penetrated the visual language of society an artist has a duty to grapple with it," went the reasoning.[9])

An art world entranced with flicker-of-the-eye effects proposed a new status for the billboard. Pop art jumped the abyss between art and advertisement as part of a defiant revision of art-world attitudes towards commercial culture. In lieu of echoing the critique of consumption that formed a staple of liberal social commentary, pop artists visually explored the consequences of mass media in the terms the advertisements themselves used.

For instance, the Muse visited James Rosenquist while he painted billboards high above Times Square. The huge scale, massive splashes of color and odd angles of viewing made his up-close painting of "realistic" body parts and products on billboards seem almost surreal. So, in his own work, collages of these types of fragments skewed viewing angles and shimmering colors became wall-sized paintings such as *F-111* (a melange of suburbia and the military-industrial complex, with a little girl baking under a hairdryer), or *I Love You with My Ford* (a car bumper, a profile, a mess of spaghetti, all lined up like a layer cake), or *President Elect* (an image of Kennedy next to a slice of Duncan Hines hyper-spongy cake, balanced on a car bumper). To ensure that his language of objects was indeed common, Rosenquist actually worked from magazine clippings he collected.[10] This point of view emphasized the functions of the viewer rather than castigating the producers of consumer culture. Public visibility was desirable and did not detract from the value of the visual. There was no longer an exclusive museum art zone where attentive looking was expected. Thus, the car-friendly pleasure zone of visual browsing came into its own.

This discussion of pop art demonstrates how consumer culture had altered the terms of visual transaction, turning what had been a rude stare into a habitual mode of seeing. A certain code of public decorum in displaying and looking was thrown on the garbage heap of civility past. Like the advertiser, the artist was targeting a "contaminated attention," one that flickered in the syntax of commercial looking. The pop artist could paint a deadpan simulation of what the auto-flâneur saw. This inactive attention could turn into a Zenlike form: mindless watching might unintentionally drop the viewer into a meditative state. In fact, in his famous 1960s TV sculptures, Nam June Paik asserted as much, going so far as to make a "TV Buddha." The thinking eye had changed: Kant's aesthetic posture of passionate contemplation bowed to the media era. In this context, billboard watching was a quintessentially sixties manner of experiencing landscape. It was noncommittal, absorbed but not reactive. It up-ended the Kantian category of passionate contemplation as *the* aesthetic attitude, and substituted for it a notion of *dispassionate* contemplation.

Given the gaudy locales framed by the windshield, the switch from the term "suburban landscape" to the more accurate term "roadside" makes sense. If we put the pop sensibility together with the gaze of the auto-flâneur, the result is an explanation of how the suburban mix of nature and commerce became customary visual fare in America. As architecture critic Reyner Banham put it, the suburbs were egalitarian and felt no compunctions about seeing the pastoral as a "landscape with figures with gadgets."[11]

In 1950s and 1960s suburbs visuality was out of control, warping customary experiences of space and time. Whether auto-flâneur, shuttle-mom, or commuter, the driver made no conscious decision to look, but inhaled a daily diet of bizarre conjunctions of nature and commerce anyway. Suburban sprawl meant traversing spaces where nothing was purely one or the other.

Suburbia saw corporations come out to the countryside with them in the 1950s and 1960s. Roadside billboards represent merely a chapter in a larger tale of this burgeoning corporate presence. Through the windshield, the auto-flâneur's gaze was one way of handling these sights. Treating the billboards as an inevitable piece of roadside garnish, this gaze was neither especially friendly nor hostile. The auto-flâneur was as unlikely to dash to the supermarket for a Swanson's TV dinner, as he was to grab a chainsaw and hack the billboard down.[12] The auto-flâneur's newly evolved codes of looking embraced contradictory responses to the suburban roadside of postwar America.

1. Ann Friedberg, *Window Shopping* (Berkeley: University of California Press, 1993) interprets visuality and modernity in a similar way using the cinema and shopping mall paradigms of looking.
2. *Essentials of Outdoor Advertising* (New York: Association of National Advertisers, 1952), 54.
3. Gwendolyn Wright, *Building the Dream: A Social History of Housing in America* (New York: Pantheon, 1981), 256.
4. Betty Friedan, *The Feminine Mystique* (New York: W W Norton, 1963).
5. See Susan Saegert, "Masculine Cities/Feminine Suburbs: Polarized Ideas, Contradictory Realities," in *Women and the American City*, ed. Catherine Stimson, et al. (Chicago: Chicago University Press, 1980), 93–108.
6. Philip Wylie, *Generation of Vipers* (New York: Rinehart, 1942), 211–14.
7. Cited in Jim Klein and Martha Olson, "Taken for a Ride," color video, 60 min. (PBS American Experience series, 1996).
8. Berman v. Parker, 348 US 26, 33 (1954) quoted in John Costonis, "Law and Aesthetics," *Michigan Law Review* 80 (January 1982), 362.
9. Susan Sontag, "Notes on Camp," *Against Interpretation, and Other Essays* (New York: Farrar, Straus & Giroux, 1964), 283–88.
10. Judy Goldman, *James Rosenquist: The Early Pictures* (New York: Gagosian Gallery/Rizzoli, 1992), 13, 14, 60, 87.
11. Reyner Banham, "The Great Gizmo," *Industrial Design* 12 (September 1965): 49.
12. Although in the 1920s, some reformers spoke of "Carrie Nationizing" the billboards, a reference to the ax-wielding temperance advocate famous for smashing the plate glass windows of saloons.

Kathleen Hulser is a historian and writer with a long-standing interest in the media. Her forthcoming book Billboard Landscapes *examines the history of conflicts over the look of the landscape, as twentieth-century corporations speckled the countryside with national advertising campaigns.*

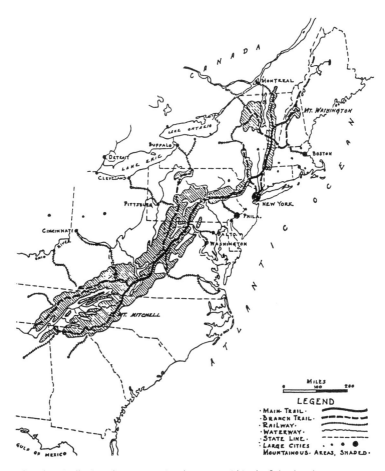

Though typically viewed as a recreational preserve within the federal park system, the Appalachian Trail, as it was originally conceived in 1921 by Benton MacKaye, was intended to be a terrestrial infrastructure that would reorganize the entire Eastern Seaboard. Because MacKaye's infrastructures were overtly expressed by the constraints of activity, they serve as rather eccentric artifacts in the contemplation of an architecture directed not by geometry or aesthetics but by timing and patterns of connectivity.

Siting Protocols
Keller Easterling

Suburban Protocols

Banality is what makes suburbia powerful. Almost everything in America is suburbia; suburbia is a distributive protocol, a code of procedures that shapes exurban development into more uniform networks of organization. The built artifacts of development systems, the highway interchange, and the suburban tract house are usually described geometrically or scrutinized aesthetically. However, their dominant architecture may be best described by the constraints governing timing, organization, and interactivity within their environments. For instance, the process of assembling some kinds of residential formations resembles agricultural production, in that large numbers of houses are executed simultaneously in uniform fields. It is the architecture, format, or protocol of that process, rather than the appearance of the suburban house, that may be the chief determinant of spatial and material consequences.

Ironically, the banality and repetition within these environments often make them responsive subjects in a discussion of active organizations. Redundancy and repetition make very fertile ground for interventions of adjustment. Like switches or fittings, these specialized sites of adjustment are the dumb components that have a powerful life either because they are multiplied across a repeated detail or intelligently positioned within a redundant or segregated environment. Empowered by connections, they may begin a process of redirecting or overwriting a context over time.

Biology, geology, mathematics, and network electronics have developed precise terms to describe active organizations and processes. For instance, biological terminology expresses relationships and duration and describes systems that evolve, "learn," or adapt over time. It describes a population of cells or neurons not by a single noun or image, but by verbs related to process and multiple time-lapse images. Similarly, at the end of the nineteenth century, geologists transferred their analytic efforts from the study of artifacts to the study of processes like fluvial activity, glaciation, and erosion, developing descriptions of watersheds or ice flows that incorporated temporal markers and notations of elastic boundary conditions. In communication and computational networks, timing and storage space are one and the same thing and so cannot be expressed in terms of absolute spaces or objects. Rather, technologists who work with these environments use the term "network architecture," to refer to the powerful protocols organizing interplay, adjustment, and timing among ecologies of circuitry.

Surprisingly, the discipline of architecture, unlike geology, biology, music, and mathematics, has very limited means of describing spatial organizations with active parts, temporal components, or differential change. Process operations are routine in architectural practice but are usually subordinated to an artistic product that has some kind of representational currency. Our culture more easily identifies and articulates static building forms.

Architects, too, are typically more fluent in descriptions of processes that are determinate or that can be named by form or geometry. In architecture's fascination with active organizations, activity is often confused with movement and has often been expressed in forms representative of dynamism. For instance, in the early twentieth century, while geologists were, in a sense, shifting their focus from nouns to verbs, from artifacts to processes, architecture was pursuing a similar fascination by stylizing motion as speed within a bachelor's world of fast cars and airplanes or fixing the activities of building with master plans and modular systems.

While contemporary discussions of active organizations often involve network thinking and computational tools, there is sometimes a stronger attraction for the representations and animations of software environments or for the computer's potential ability to design complexity than for the architecture of network processes and interplay behind the screen. However, activity and motion are not the same, and the attempt to gain a comprehensive understanding of spatial systems does not take advantage of their power. The most powerful and perhaps the only architecture within an active organization involves not its control but its adjustment and the amplification of that adjustment within a connected organization.

Many of America's developmental organizations thrive on both dominant formats and opportunistic exceptions, and are, through consumption, vehicles of the very inventions of their adjustment. While most of those adjustments are accidental and self-reinforcing, some eccentric episodes in the history of exurban development use existing organizations to generate truly alternative development protocols.

Linear Infrastructure

Though typically viewed as a recreational preserve within the federal park system, the Appalachian Trail, as it was originally conceived in 1921, was intended to be a terrestrial infrastructure that would reorganize the entire Eastern Seaboard. It, rather than the metropolis, would become the central spine of development, reversing the dominant pattern of concentric development around metropolitan areas. The Appalachians, as a reservoir of natural resources, would locate and direct industry and community independent of the big city.

The interstate geological formation of the Appalachian Ridge would function as a kind of public utility working in parallel with waterways and other transportation and hydroelectrical networks. This 2000-mile mediating line from Maine to Georgia would travel through similar crest line terrain at its interior, and vastly different terrain at its periphery. By its placement, this linear order also inverted the typical hierarchy of transportation and development infrastructure. In the typical arrangement, long-distance rail and highways formed the main transportation trunks. Primary, secondary, and tertiary streets branched from these, and led to pedestrian networks. Conversely, in the trail arrangement, a footpath was the dominant infrastructure that organized streets and rails. Branch lines of the trail and special railways would extend this landscape into thirty-six large metropolitan areas surrounding the trail. An infrastructure of land, a "Super National" forest, and a network of compact communities and industries would crystallize around the footpath.[1] This network of regional cities would replace the suburbs and be differentiated by diverse locations, industries, and resources. The trail essentially proposed a linear ordering principle and a unit of industry and community for a new economy. It would broadcast a field of influence and a new mechanism for production and distribution as well as for migrations of population.

The trail was typical of the infrastructure projects designed by Benton MacKaye, a forester, regional planner, and self-proclaimed "geotechnician." MacKaye proposed large linear infrastructures that followed geological features, such as the crest line of a mountain range or a river valley. He developed several national and international prototypes in, for example, the Tennessee River Valley, the Mohawk Valley, and Alaska, though the Appalachian Trail is the best known of these. MacKaye also proposed one of the initial conceptions of the limited access highway, which, in his formulations, was also to operate as a terrestrial infrastructure.

More interesting than MacKaye's somewhat holistic social prescriptions was the way in which he constituted the sites of intervention within the spaces and operations of active organizations. MacKaye said of planning, "finally the thing planned is not mere area or land, but movement or activity."[2]

MacKaye's Geotechnics

Because MacKaye's infrastructures were overtly expressed by the constraints of activity, they serve as rather eccentric artifacts in the contemplation of an architecture directed not by geometry or aesthetics but by timing and patterns of connectivity. One of the pretenses associated with some contemporary notions of network is that they are the most sophisticated in a succession of cultural conclusions that subsume a narrower range of thought. MacKaye, however, referenced a variety of models for active organizations in a way that favored the coexistence rather than succession of ideas. He found new sites of intervention by transposing geological models of activity and process onto a spatial environment. He also found new sites within an active and consciously crafted virtual environment. Both geology and mental/perceptual processes had their own operatives and constructs that described a kind of ecology or architecture of interplay. MacKaye used both of these models to format space and perceptions of space to reveal the activity and exchange within an environment. He "discovered" expanses of space within these processes and within new arrangements of perceptions.

Terrestrial landscapes are often associated with visual beauty, spiritual reverie and environmentalism. Environmentalism and even the word "environment" are associated with conservation and protection. The word "ecology" has even become synonymous with environmentalism. The environmental movement generally traces a continuous history between the ideologies of turn-of-the-century conservation and the emotional messages of the ecological crisis of the 1960s and 1970s. However MacKaye's science of "geotechnics" represents a prescient intervening episode. MacKaye was among the first to use the word "environment," but his use fills the term with a much richer philosophical tradition than its current understanding, and his philosophy marks an unusual cross reference between the sentiments of the technocracy movement and the environmental movement. MacKaye's philosophy seems to be cloaked in a similar kind of emotional rhetoric with holistic projections. However his work was not primarily focused on the preservation and appreciation of plants, animals, and landscapes, but rather on the exploration and manipulation of a *technological* ecology.

MacKaye wrote that the term "geotechnics" fused into one the words "geography, forestry and conservation, engineering, colonization, regional planning, and economics."[3] He promoted a kind of composite engineering wherein land-based sciences and engineering were on an equal footing. He was a self-proclaimed "regional planner" when planning was a relatively new endeavor. Though regional planning would typically be the task of committees and official agencies, MacKaye was fashioning the role for a single practitioner. Different in intent from planning practices that evolved within the design professions, MacKaye's approach was ecological in nature, that is, it was a part of some interplay or exchange that was not always direct, traceable, or predictable. Perhaps because of his background in the earth sciences and forestry, he treated a site as an environment of interdependent parts. Within these ecologies, adjustments remotely activate each other and small shifts in balance or orientation have enormous effect. Connectivity rendered the tactical move effective and made possible some kind of remote activation between parts.

Geological Models

MacKaye studied geology and geography at Harvard University in the late nineteenth century, when those disciplines were shifting focus away from the study of mineral artifacts toward the study of physiography and the activity of global land forms. Like biological terminology, geological and geographical terms of study began to focus on expressions of relationship, duration, and organization within such things as fluvial movements, erosion, glaciation, and metamorphosis.

Man's activities were considered to be a part of these larger movements. MacKaye often expressed the outcomes of his interventions as continuations of this geological movement, and he analyzed aspects of human geography in terms usually reserved for terrestrial activity. Man's manipulations of industry and technology were seen as a form of nature rather than a system that necessarily dominated nature. At a time when technology was being used as a means of galvanizing politics around very deterministic principles, MacKaye expressed technology in terms of a fluid ecology. He treated the industrial landscape like a wilderness or like a fluvial system that could be diverted or constrained. Later in his career he wrote, "Geotechnics consists of emulating nature."[4]

Sampling intelligence from biological, geological, and fluvial systems, MacKaye proposed adjustable national and international terrestrial infrastructures that would revalue and redirect other infrastructures of rail and highway as well as reconfigure exurban communities. He used words like "levee" and "watershed" to describe the behavior of his infrastructures. The trail network would contain and direct or divert certain kinds of development. Fluvial models allowed MacKaye to consider an elastic boundary condition that was active over a long duration. His infrastructures were intended to remagnetize and re-center development in the territories through which they passed. They would work as "levees" or governors, able to change their own constitution as well as regulate change within a larger environment over time.

The qualitative terms that MacKaye assigned to the Appalachian network are telling. One of the most important qualities of these new sites of intervention was their power as partial or tactical interventions. Since the sites were constituted within patterns of connection and process, population flows, transportation and utility networks, and other distributive protocols, small adjustments effected the larger whole. The footpath, scaled to the body within a single section, became a powerful mark or divide in the land when extended for hundreds of miles.

Within recognized patterns of connectivity certain operatives were reciprocal or part of some exchange. Though not generally regarded as a constructive architectural tool, subtraction performed with an awareness of the possible response or release of other active surrounding parts was used as a positive space-making device. The network operated by remote activation and subtraction, rearranging populations in sites some distance from the spine. A process of incremental subtraction would change the urban order from a series of concentric nodes to a distributed network straddling a spine.

After attaining a gigantic length, the trail was no longer simple. It was not a single trail but a "cobweb"5 of trails that would cover the mountain. As it intersected other infrastructure networks, it would create new branches and circuits. MacKaye portrayed the trail as a cross-environmental arrangement between several separate ecologies. It would become a kind of differential filter to organize activities within both terrestrial and technological ecologies. It would transfer and deliver people and resources between a metropolitan world and a primeval or indigenous world, and between different forms of conveyance. Modest spatial changes had a radiating effect, so that even though the Appalachian Trail was mammoth in size, it remained a tactical adjustment. It initiated a process of systemic though not necessarily comprehensive changes with an outcome that was not entirely predictable.

Virtual Models

MacKaye developed geotechnics as a cultural practice that he called the "art of developing environment." He advanced a complex methodology for the instrumental use of mental craft in merging ecologies of land with ecologies of consciousness, and in so doing intended to produce a kind of cultural space. His approach was particularly unusual in that he considered this craft to be useful to both planning and engineering. It is this approach to practice and its comfortable coexistence with technical expertise that may be the most provocative aspect of his work.

According to MacKaye's mental craft, contemplation was prompted by physical activity. Physical passage through the landscape (walking, riding, etc.) was a mnemonic for both recalling and storing experience. When MacKaye used the term "environment" he referred to the enlarged stage of the enveloping outdoors. (MacKaye's father was an actor, a director of theatrical spectacles, and an inventor of stage machinery.) Environment was the surrounding medium of immaterial culture and material civilization. Passage along the trail was expanded beyond simple visual contact with the scenery. From a high altitude, the view was enlarged, and within the narrow path many historical epochs were collapsed into a single body and a single moment. The panoramic view of a valley, with its different soils, vegetation, and landscape features, prompted a survey of geological/biological cycles and human migrations. MacKaye proposed looking long enough to see, in time lapse, a slowly animating landscape—to see not the still but the motion picture.

"Visualizing" involved an abstract reappraisal of the environment that incorporated ideas about knowing through seeing, seeing through thinking, and perceiving haptically by perceiving optically. Intellectual understanding was deepened through a kind of enhanced perception, and perception was enhanced not through powers of magnification but through powers of time.

SITING PROTOCOLS

Action was understood to foster a kind of elastic trajectory through memory, which was built by and reciprocally affected the perception of matter outside of the mind. The parallel environment of the mind was brought into contact with the landscape in a kind of willed overlay. The practice engaged the mind and the body in summoning multiple scenarios over time. This cross pollination of intelligence provided a rich inventory of material for problem solving. MacKaye's philosophy was either directly or indirectly influenced by Ralph Waldo Emerson, Henry David Thoreau, and American pragmaticists, but it strongly resembled Sir Patrick Geddes's interpretations of Henri Bergson's work in its reliance on the use of memory and eidetic perceptions. In a way, his practice illustrated many Bergsonian concepts about the instrumentality of action in stimulating the mind. MacKaye's approach also strongly resembles an actor's mental craft within which a virtual world is intentionally constructed and a mental or physical cue is used to store and release experiences and rhythms in the body.

MacKaye consciously shaped mental systems into virtual space within which understanding and interplay were multiplied without conscious control. The exercise of perception and virtual cross-reference was a precipitant of action. Just as the mind was born into or discovered in haptic and optic contact, so perception was born into and colored by the mind's memory. MacKaye placed equal emphasis on that virtual landscape and its reciprocal analog in the real. He identified three classes of natural resources:

1) Material resources (soils, forest, metallic ores). 2) Energy resources (the mechanical energy resident in falling water, coal seams, and other natural elements). 3) Psychological resources (the human psychological energy, or happiness, resident in a natural setting or environment).[6]

The latent power of the environment as mined and "converted" by the artist was like the latent power in waterfalls and dams. It was, like electricity, an "outward flow" of energy.

To effect change in this environment did not necessarily involve physical restructuring. MacKaye imagined that simply positioning observers on the crest line gave them a chance to envision the land rather than the metropolis as a commanding order. Mountains replaced the city's tall buildings as the architecture of height from which to view development. Thus a carefully placed vantage point and a simple set of narratives adjusted the most instant and immaterial component of the land, that is, the cultural persuasions that influence its perception. Finally, the trail was immaterial. The trail was really only a marking of order or a line of force, not a construction. It was a void that would redirect the use of a large expanse of space, a virtual adjustment of the protocols of culture and industry. The shift proposed by the Appalachian Trail was a shift in center, and that new center was actually a vacant "openway." Vacancy in this case meant the removal of dominant controls or a condition within which the landscape was allowed to exist in the absence of prevailing development forces.

MacKaye also thought that the effort to build such a trail would begin to merge with other national efforts on a similar scale. Large infrastructure projects resembled, for instance, warfare in scale, equipment, and manpower. MacKaye proposed his infrastructure projects in relation to wartime efforts or postwar employment, but he also proposed the projects as a possible substitute for the nation's attraction to the drama of military efforts. He merged the infrastructure projects with forestry, community building, highway development, water control, and dam building efforts as well. For instance, he developed a formulation about the trail in relation to electrical and automobile networks. MacKaye's own contemplative process joined the protocols of production and distribution, allowing him to express the attributes of an economy in terms of its "psychic resources" and adjust that environment by adjusting a virtual as well as physical site.

Siting Protocols
MacKaye's craft is significant especially when viewed within the context of our contemporary development environments, where protocols of process rather than formal manipulations are the dominant architecture. Whatever the content of his prescriptions, he was an inventor of development protocols, an artist whose medium was the active processes that remain largely unexpressed in the fields of design and planning. MacKaye

proposed that infrastructure be composed as a terrestrial transportation or utility network, and he proposed that that network become a protocol for an ongoing active function. It was this protocol—reliant on a position in space and in cultural thought—that was the actual site of intervention. But that position was constructed by highlighting a carefully selected existing condition. MacKaye's adjustment of activities and immaterial cultural persuasions potentially generated enormous material consequences. The craft was reliant on the invisible and ephemeral, and on the worlds within the body and mind. Through a kind of extreme form of resourcefulness, he proposed to operate within the protocols of distribution and persuasion that are the true, if sometimes accidental, realms of power and influence in America.

1. Benton MacKaye, "Great Appalachian Trail from New Hampshire to the Carolinas," *New York Times*, Sunday, 18 February 1923.
2. Benton MacKaye, "Regional Planning and Ecology," *Ecological Monographs* 10 (July 1940): 349.
3. MacKaye, "Great Appalachian Trail," 40.
4. Benton MacKaye, "Global Law," *The Survey* 87 (June 1951): 268.
5. Benton MacKaye, "Progress Toward the Appalachian Trail," *Appalachia* 15 (December 1922): 244.
6. Ibid., 50–51.

Keller Easterling is an architect and writer living in New York City. Her research concerns American infrastructure protocols as understood through the study of other kinds of networks and active organizations.

Icons of the Sprawl
Kevin Miller

ICONS OF THE SPRAWL

ICONS OF THE SPRAWL

Kevin Miller is a photographer in New York City.

KEVIN MILLER   37

The Suburban Canon Over Time

Paul H. Mattingly

The 1980 United States Federal Census corroborated that more Americans live in suburbs than in rural or urban areas. Yet, "suburbia" regularly receives a ritualized critical scrutiny from scholars, journalists, and media commentators as a deleterious cultural force: smug, homogenized, oppressively middle-class, self-indulgent, and indifferent to its destructive impact on the city. Suburbia has become more than a convenient foil to explain urban decay and a culture of narcissism; it has become a cultural canon that often resists contextual data supporting a different perspective and a different landscape.[1] How did such a disparaging image arise about the most popular form of American residential and communal life?

Suburbanization is as old as urbanization; the two phenomena arose together. In the days of Chaucer the suburbs were dangerous places, fit for outcasts and brigands; only in the nineteenth century did the city's margins become, if not desirable, at least experimental, exercises in a reintegration of managed nature and urban amenities. Even in these early experimental stages suburbs were not the wholly controlled plaything of the rich but accommodated all classes in varying proportions. In spite of the much-discussed differences between suburban idylls and the modern metropolis, early commentators general-

Levittown, New York

ly assumed a mutual dependence of each on the other. The clichéd differences between "country" and "city" in the nineteenth century were not as sharp as the twentieth-century distinctions between "suburb" and "city."[2]

These time-bound variations underscore one of the key omissions of our current suburban canon: the American suburb is no longer regularly viewed as a historical construct that changes over time. The easy invocation of post-World War II Levittowns, as if their initial sameness stood for all suburbanization, has obscured the multiple communities they have represented. Indeed even Levittowns have metamorphosed into individualized architectural styles over time.

How is the current polarizing canon formed by both scholarly and popular analyses of suburban culture? Until very recently historians and social scientists blithely invoked the language of "individualism," of "middle class," and of "community" in referring to the suburbs, as if such terms possessed special analytic powers.[3] The canon seemed to coerce the scholars' questions and focused attention on the patterns of the community's elite and affluent middle class, as if they alone provide the guidance and leadership to town initiatives. Journalists joined the discourse, pleased to document all manner of "escapes" from city crime, decay of infrastructure, and recent immigrants. They now feign surprise to discover social ills in suburbia, as if the suburbs have now entered a new phase that opens them for the first time to city problems.[4]

Two principle problems of the canon have interfered with a critical engagement with the American suburb. First, commentaries on suburban behavior are generally intramural; they remain within the community under scrutiny and take for granted the protective isolation that its residents purportedly seek. As a consequence, few histories of these communities address a common set of issues that might generate comparisons, distinctions, and general patterns in spite of differences.[5] Second, the evidence of most suburban studies ignores testimony of suburbanites themselves and concentrate on the published perceptions of urban planners, architects, realtors, politicians, and publishers, whose careers are invariably dominated by urban issues. This urban bias treats the suburb as something other, something distanced, a critical target understood through aerial photographs (such as the frontispiece).[6]

Elements of the canon appear even in Kenneth Jackson's prize-winning *Crabgrass Frontier,* a historical study that made a substantive contribution to our understanding of suburbanization. While Jackson convincingly argued about the distinctive role of the federal government in the development of postwar suburbs,[7] he relapsed into the canon and blamed the suburbs for the city's decay. He did not probe the cultural impact of the federal intervention (did federal intervention change suburbanite priorities?) or the self-destructive policies of the city's own leadership (at what point did urban policy initiatives seriously alarm an urban middle class and cause "flight" problems attributed to suburbia?). Jackson's new perspective on suburbia could not prevail over the canon's habit of scapegoating the suburbs.

Jackson synthesized a large and scattered literature and made abundantly clear how much our knowledge of suburbanization relies on popular, idealized conceptions disseminated through mass magazines, themselves predominantly produced in urban environments. The notion of "the romantic suburb" is based on such media and in select suburbs is a reality. For example, much has been made of one of the oldest American suburbs, Llewellyn Park in New Jersey. But few discussions actually trace the transformation from the original prospectus of the community through the realization of its functioning social structure. Rather, critics stay with the original prospectus, noting the planned privacy and individuation and the use of nature to seclude and isolate, rather than ask about the social problems that inform the maturation of the community. The very assumptions about "community formation" have become matters of intellectual debate rather than complicated, historical negotiations among actual residents with different perspectives and different social classes.

It is remarkable how many case studies of suburban communities have been completed without a serious engagement with the oral history of suburbanites. Not one interviewee in a recent study of Leonia, New Jersey characterized their move to suburbia as "flight," the ubiquitous metaphor of media and scholarship. As John Stilgoe's *Borderland* has forcefully argued, suburban residents in the main do not depart the city to "escape" from something but rather because they are going to something.[8] In addition, while oral histories of suburbanites regularly corroborate this sentiment, they also manifest an enormous range of viewpoints. Indeed neighbors' expectations of differences are more readily found than their cultivation of homogeneity. There is enough evidence from the testimony of suburban dwellers, even allowing for a reverse romanticizing, to question the assumption of both "fleedom" and homogeneity in the American suburb. For example, census data show that class, ethnic, and racial variety of some of New York's suburbs matches that within the city, especially before World War II.

Yet even in those suburbs where the affluent form the core, critics need to consider the relative power of the nonaffluent in shaping the suburban landscape.[9] The interaction of distinct social classes needs to become a priority in interpreting suburbia. How this interaction changes over time has everything to do with the suburb's interaction with the city, a dynamic that pervades every suburb. The crucial feature of this seminal interaction is its historical nature; how each social class grouping changes over time illuminates a largely omitted dimension of the current suburban canon.

Only recently have scholars attempted a chronological schema for American suburbanization, a consequence of little scholarly inquiry into the suburb before the 1970s. If the auto provided the contextual technology for mass suburbanization after the New Deal, how did earlier technology, especially in transportation, contribute to suburban development? Sam Bass Warner's seminal 1962 history, *Streetcar Suburbs*, examined the impact of trolleys and found that they fostered social class divisions.[10] The less affluent resided close to the noisy trolleys, the more affluent at some remove. Warner thus laid the grounds for a greater social class consciousness in approaching suburbs. In addition, he registered a bracing suspicion of the idealized plans that construct any community. Yet Warner did not examine how suburbanites organized their social or political lives. Exactly how did the trolley technology—if it indeed represented a distinctive stage of growth—reshape suburbia's values?[11] Exactly how did suburban residents respond to these emergent social class divisions?

Warner studied his Massachusetts examples only for the years 1870 to 1900. The full impact of the trolley's history was so foreshortened that no clear directing could be made for the earlier dominance of the commuter railroad or the later auto era. A longer view, matching each of these technologies with shifting social structures within a single suburb, would begin to establish the suburb as a formative but distinctive force over time. Most suburbs arose within an existing social and cultural matrix, in which city influences made themselves felt. Many early suburban communities, even those with affluent railroad commuters, had residents who were neither affluent nor commuters. Indeed such a mixture of social classes was essential if the affluent were to be attracted to nonurban settings; the affluent expected services and amenities, provided by less affluent classes, commensurate with urban expectations. Even when social classes did not mix, each social group shaped distinctive social organizations and cultural traditions.

During the trolley stage of suburban development, roughly 1870–1930 (overlapping the auto stage), there were, as Warner found, geographical differentiations to match emergent social class divisions. Generally, these divisions were more complex than those in earlier suburbs. The trolley's nickel fare did preclude some working-class people, but it also made inexpensive housing available to many employees of the burgeoning corporations in the city. The trolley's appearance occurred simultaneously with a geometric expansion of the American middle class.[12] The result was a stratification of society, but its divisions were largely within a ballooning middle-class pool whose strata were more permeable than those within the elite or the working class. Compared to the railroad stage before it and the auto stage afterward, the trolley gave the American suburb its most democratic moment.

Such democracy was also reflected in the style of suburban houses. Most older suburbs did produce private houses ranging from small and large Queen Anne cottages to homes in a variety of colonial and Tudor styles. But these styles rarely dominated a community. In most turn-of-the-century suburbs the homes were largely built by small local jobbers who most often constructed variations on a basic farmstead style or adapted a design from the house builder books and blueprints in the new mass magazines.[13] Most jobbers could expand or contract their basic blueprint to fit the family's income, leaving out a wall here, adding a porch or window there. In most turn-of-the-century suburbs some sections gradually assumed a veneer of prestige over other sections, but in many sections there were great variations of style and class.

In this context of the mix of social classes, some suburban commentators have begun to reconsider the hitherto stylized treatment of both gender and race. Much of these discussions have been based on articles about the suburban family from *The Ladies Home Journal, Cosmopolitan,* or *The Saturday Evening Post.* Historians have debated whether the new domestic technology of refrigerators and vacuum cleaners further chained women to the domestic hearth or liberated them. However, in most early suburbs women's volunteer work outside the home created the suburb's most powerful community agencies. Voluntary activity and even employment within one's suburban boundaries were often characterized as "helping out a neighbor," thus muting how transformational the work actually was. Twentieth-century notions of domesticity, as Dolores Hayden rightly insists, sustained assumptions of its nineteenth-century inheritance far longer than many observers thought,[14] but, I would add, domesticity by the early twentieth century had come to mean something very different, for both good and ill. In the twentieth century the language of domesticity became the sleeve through which women's activity extended beyond the home. At times, "helping a neighbor" opened salaried work to women whose husbands refused to have them "work" in the city.

As suburban commentators have begun to reexamine gender, so too they are rethinking race. African-American enclaves could be found in turn-of-the-century suburbs, especially in areas of the northeast, like Bergen County, New Jersey, where they have long had a presence. Suburban studies using census data have been surprised to find African Americans at all before World War II and assumed they must be domestics. In actuality a small percentage of New York City's suburban population in 1900 were African Americans, and many of these were not domestics. Though the African-American community was small, one must also consider the social organizations it created, especially the churches, which often established a social structure and attraction for later incoming residents. Indeed when African Americans migrated from rural southern communities in substantial numbers during and after World War I, they often found cities unattractive and settled in outlying suburbs for the same quasi-rural features that induced their white neighbors.[15] The earlier arrivals to Leonia, a New Jersey suburb of New York City, often resided in "integrated" neighborhoods, much more so than later suburban stages permitted.

The active presence of women and African Americans in suburbia clearly undermines the present suburban canon. So too does the presence of immigrants, whom the canon often suggests were the cause of urban flight. In Leonia foreign-born suburbanites composed nearly one-third of household heads in 1880 and only slipped to one-quarter by 1920. During the same period nearly half of Leonia's household heads had foreign-born fathers. In addition, the putative power of the homeownership ideal seemed less powerful than it is sometimes assumed. In 1900 forty-seven percent of the residents of Leonia were renters; only fifteen percent owned their homes. By 1920 thirty percent still rented, while only seventeen percent owned homes. Margaret Marsh's *Suburban Lives* discovered analogous percentages in the Philadelphia suburb of Haddonfield, New Jersey.[16] Rather than follow the canon and take ownership as a given, Marsh questioned when the ideal of homeownership became a practiced ideal.

The canon's simplistic association of suburbia with homeownership becomes less defensible once the suburban experience is subjected to historical and cultural scrutiny. Over time, precisely what have suburbanites sought in their move to suburbia?[17] There is no question that the rhetoric of family and privacy arise but often fail to encompass the full meaning of suburbia for those living there. Spectators have become overly preoccupied with urban/suburban differences (like apartments versus single-family homes) and with domestic architecture. But they seldom probe the nature of values in the suburbs. Within the canon the language of analysis, even for astute commentators, generally revolves around the terms "nostalgia" and "mythology." Nostalgia often follows from the prevalence of "colonial" architecture from the 1920s onward, and mythology, connoting fanciful misperceptions of reality, attaches to the sense of security that lawn, hedging, and fences accord the suburban landscape.

Both "nostalgia" and "mythology" have become devices for disowning the suburban past. The actual style of the American suburb has become extraordinary elastic over the past few decades, often ignoring the colonial predominance, encompassing everything from early bungalows and Cape Cods to expansive center-hall plan styles. One recent study detailed ten different styles within the American suburb but awkwardly admitted each style's "overlapping" characteristic in an effort to define the distinctive suburban landscape.[18] Rather than impose generic models, we need to explore the plurality of architectural styles in terms of residents' values, as much as those of the architects and building contractors. The supply-side approach to material culture is one more aspect of the canon that precludes engagement with the actual suburbanites and their aspirations. There really has been no evidence to establish that a colonial style documents a defensive atavism for the American suburb. In fact immigrants to suburbia, like immigrants to the turn-of-the-century city, coveted the colonial style as often as native-born suburbanites. The colonial style seemed to represent to both longtime residents and newcomers a common ground and an affirmation of joint commitments to the community.

Similarly the ubiquitous and largely unstudied phenomenon of voluntary organizations in suburban socialization has confused the sources of power in suburban politics. In older suburbs local initiatives provided the stimulus to a great range of constructive, community-enhancing projects: theater productions, tree-plantings, literary and artistic endeavors, fund raisers for schools and churches, adult education, sports and leisure activities, and other forms of mutual improvement. To be fair, many city neighborhoods had parallel projects. But these endeavors in suburbia are so reflexively characterized as middle class—as if automatically all middle-class suburbanites have "leisure time"—that suburban inquiries rarely ask how suburban middle-class experiences differ from those in the city. Even

THE SUBURBAN CANON OVER TIME

to question the middle-class experience is to confront the myopia of the suburban canon, which equates the rise of suburbia with the flight of the middle class. Oddly critics do not mention reverse flight, when suburbanites return to live in the city. The canon has impeded any inquiry into the nature of the twentieth-century middle class and has so wedded the middle class to the suburb that one wonders whether any middle class remain in the city.

This ahistorical isolation of the American suburb begins to break down when notions of class, gender, and race are connected to patterns of work. Historian Robert Fishman has provocatively argued that America in the late twentieth century has gravitated into a post-suburban stage and an unprecedented form of the American city.[19] His argument rests largely on patterns of interaction between suburb and city, particularly with regard to work. The postmodern suburb, Fishman argues, is less dependent on the city for jobs, more likely to send its residents to adjacent counties and towns than the city for work, and more self-contained in terms of available goods and services. Ultimately whole regions are united into supercities, like Silicon Valley in California and Tyson's Corner, once a Virginia suburb of Washington DC. The result is a new configuration—not urban, not rural, not suburban, but a combination of all three.

Fishman's arguments raise questions that require examination of suburbanization and urbanization simultaneously rather than in isolation. He has exercised great imagination in projecting the consequences of a new interactive suburban pattern of work and transit. Still, Fishman's arguments reflect features of the canon. First, he overrelies on planners' conceptions of suburbia, as if no changes occurred in their implementation. Second, some of his "new" interactive features of residence, work, and travel are actually not so new. Third, his fascination with suburban metamorphoses needs to credit the force of each community's past and inherited patterns. Part of the power of the megalopolis he constructs depends on a false history of the polarization of city and suburb.

We do not yet have a firm understanding of how similar or different the experiences of suburban and urban residents actually were. We also have failed to consider how mobile or rooted groups were in either locus over time. We are beginning to gain some sense that older suburbs stabilized themselves via families who continued in a single locus for multiple generations. In virtually every older suburb, many residents did not join their commuting neighbors to the metropolis but were employed locally or regionally. Yet no one has examined city dwellers who found employment outside the city because of transportation advances in the heyday of suburbanization.[20]

The suburban canon has dramatically affected our assumptions about the "modern suburb." Fishman has voiced his suspicions that the new megalopolis—he has characterized it as a "technoburb"—will displace the suburb as we now know it. But like so many students of suburban planners, architects, developers, and media proponents with urban perspectives on suburbia, Fishman has taken little stock in the actual experience of the American suburb.[21] Suburban communities, especially those that support many voluntary organizations, will always contain some vestiges of the past (like "neighborliness") that residents are not willing to forego for the sake of "modernization." This voluntary culture accommodates the different priorities of its residents by keeping goals clear and differences subdued. Inevitably some of the driving forces of these informal organizations are the older residents of the town (not necessarily the most affluent, as the canon would have it). These citizens provide an insistent continuity with the past and have insured that any "modernization" to their communities respects certain valued traditions. They shun the idea that progress necessitates a repudiation of the past or an unprecedented embrace of the future. However within the framework of the canon, such behavior is labeled "conservative," "defensive," "self-interested," and "unmodern."

Fishman has identified a new stage of "suburbanization" that arose in the 1960s and early 1970s and that resulted from an explosion in the number of two-career households. Such households not only provided select elements of economic stability but also made the voluntary culture of suburbia more difficult to sustain, which has increased the significance of formal political and governmental operations as a device of social problem solving. Before the 1960s the formal governmental structure of a community depended on citizen's volunteer work and their commitment to community life. Even in one-party suburbs, politics were usually subordinated to the power of voluntary organizations and the informal decision making of a few select individuals. After the 1960s political leaders and their campaigns not only distanced themselves from the suburb's voluntary culture, they became, in many suburbanites' eyes, more contentious and ideological, that is, less "harmonious," less "neighborly." Among many suburban residents, it was not antiurban "nostalgia" to insist upon the attractive days of "country town" life; it was an effort to inject some historical controls on unfamiliar political practices in suburban life.[22]

To understand the full history of suburbia is to collect the oral history of the suburban community. The seminal task here goes beyond mere data collection; it involves the reconstruction of a community's priorities and the ways in which they participated in the shaping of the community's collective memory.[23] In the process observers will find truths countervailing, even diametrically opposed, to those we have hitherto trusted as the essential windows on suburban life. The suburbanites' sense of history, however accurate or inaccurate according to the experts' views, is one of the compelling forces in community formation and socialization. The images of history, cherished by suburban towns, have sometimes resulted in forceful, even unlawful covenants and zoning practices against individuals and groups,[24] but they have also underscored the power of social iconography, which social scientists have too often caricatured and dismissed. The suburbanites' own sense of history, both as information and mentality, provides a window not only into old but into new suburban landscapes. In the process of reengaging that history, one displaces the myopic canon that has deflected our understanding of the American suburb over time.[25]

1. Kenneth Jackson, "America's Rush to Suburbia," *New York Times*, 9 July 1996, 15. Jackson is the author of the most comprehensive and respected historical study of the suburbs to date, *The Crabgrass Frontier: The Suburbanization of the United States* (New York: Oxford University Press, 1985). See also Zane Miller, *Suburb: Neighborhood and Community in Forest Park, Illinois 1935–1976* (Knoxville, TN: University of Tennessee Press, 1981).

2. See Raymond Williams, *The Country and the City* (New York: Oxford University Press, 1973).

3. See John Archer, "Ideology and Aspiration: Individualism, the Middle Class, and the Genesis of the Anglo-American suburb," *Journal of Urban History* vol. 14, no. 2 (February 1988): 214–53.

4. See Diana Jean Schemo, "Facing Big-City Problems: L.I. Suburbs Try to Adapt," *New York Times*, 16 March 1994, A1. This was the first of two articles grouped under the byline "Tarnished Haven." See also Esther B. Fein, "Empty Lawns: Aging in the Suburbs," *New York Times*, 19 July 1994, A1, B5.

5. One notable exception is Michael Ebner, *Creating Chicago's North Shore: A Suburban History* (Chicago: University of Chicago Press, 1988).

6. For an excellent overview of this bias and the relevant literature, see Margaret Marsh, "Reconsidering the Suburbs: An Exploration of Suburban Historiography," *Pennsylvania Magazine of History and Biography* vol. 112, no. 4 (October 1988): 579–605.

7. For numerous, discussible features of this postwar stage of suburbanization, see Barbara Kelly, ed., *Suburbia Re-examined* (Westport, CT: Greenwood Press, 1989).

8. John Stilgoe, *Borderland: Origins of the American Suburb, 1820–1939* (New Haven: Yale University Press, 1988).

9. Ibid. See also David Contosta, *Suburb in the City: Chestnut Hill, Philadelphia, 1850–1990* (Columbus, OH: Ohio State University Press, 1992), a recent study, executed with superb detail and important factual discoveries, that describes Chestnut Hill, Pennsylvania as systematically divided and controlled by a few select affluent families. The working-class residents, who have been meticulously documented, have only a passive role on community dynamics. The result is an oversubscription to an image of "the romantic suburb." See also the fine study, Carol A. O'Connor, *A Sort of Utopia: Scarsdale, 1891–1981* (Albany: SUNY Albany Press, 1983), which for all its merits becomes a story of upper-middle-class trajectory.

10. Sam Bass Warner, *Streetcar Suburbs* (Boston: Athenaeum, 1962).

11. Ibid. See also Steven J. Hoffman, " 'A Plan of Quality:' The Development of Mt. Lebanon, a 1920s Automobile Suburb," *Journal of Urban History* vol. 18, no. 2 (February 1992): 141ff.

12. Stuart M. Blumin, *The Emergence of the Middle Class: Social Experiences in the American City, 1760–1900* (Cambridge: Cambridge University Press, 1989).

13. James Wunsch, "The Suburban Cliché," *Journal of Social History* vol. 28, no. 3 (Spring 1995): 644–58.

14. Dolores Hayden, *Redesigning the American Dream: The Future of Housing, Work and Family Life* (New York: W W Norton, 1984).

15. Leslie E. Wilson and Valerie S. Hartman, "The Other Migration: The Foundations of African-American Suburban Settlement, 1880–1930," in Joseph F. Richel, ed., *American Cities and Towns: Historical Perspectives* (Pittsburgh: Duquesne

University Press, 1992), 67–95. See also Andrew Weise, "Places of Our Own: Suburban Black Towns Before 1960," *Journal of Urban History* vol. 19. no 3 (May 1993): 30–54 and Harold X. Connolly, "Black Movements into the Suburbs," *Urban Affairs Quarterly* 9 (September 1993): 19–111.

16. Margaret Marsh, *Suburban Lives* (New Brunswick, NJ: Rutgers University Press, 1990).

17. Henry C. Binford, *The First Suburbs: Residential Communities on the Boston Periphery, 1815–1860* (Chicago: University of Chicago Press, 1984) and Clifford Edward Clark, *The American Family Home, 1800–1860* (Chapel Hill, NC: University of North Carolina Press, 1886) have done important work in citing cultural values in the context of technology as a primary force in suburbanization. See also Marsh, "Reconsidering the Suburbs," 598–99.

18. Susan Mulchahey Chase, David L. Ames, and Rebecca Siders, *Suburbanization in the Vicinity of Wilmington, Delaware, 1880–1950: A Historic Context* (Newark, DE: Center for Historic Architecture and Engineering, University of Delaware, 1992), especially chapter 3.

19. Robert Fishman, "America's New City: Megalopolis Unbound," *Wilson Quarterly* 14 (Winter 1990): 25–48; see also Fishman's important study, *Bourgeois Utopias: The Rise and Fall of Suburbia* (New York: Basic Books, 1987). For a stimulating presentation of the postmodern suburb in a postmodern key, see John Dorst, *The Written Suburb: An American Site, An Ethnographic Dilemma* (Philadelphia: University of Pennsylvania Press, 1989).

20. See Herbert J. Gans, "Urbanism and Suburbanism as Ways of Life: A Re-evaluation of Definitions," in Alexander B. Callow, Jr., *American Urban History* (New York: Oxford University Press, 1969), 504–18 for a still insightful treatment of the similarities and differences in our city and suburban assumptions.

21. An important exception to this generalization is Miller, *Suburb*.

22. Michael Birkner, *A Country Town No More: The Transformation of Begenfield, New Jersey, 1894–1994* (Rutherford, NJ: Fairleigh Dickinson University Press, 1994).

23. Michael Frisch, "The Memory of History," in *Presenting the Past*, ed. Susan Porter Benson, Steven Brier, and Roy Rosenzweig (Philadelphia: Temple University Press, 1986); see also David Thelan, "Memory and American History," *Journal of American History* vol. 75, no. 4 (March 1989): 1117 ff.

24. See Ellen Skinner, *A Social History of Planning and Land Use: White Plains, New York, 1900–1972* (Ph.D. Dissertation, New York University, 1990).

25. Much of my thinking about this entire problem—a social canon overwhelming a sense of history—has evolved out of my own study, *Suburban Landscapes: Politics and Culture in a Metropolitan Community*, publication forthcoming.

Paul H. Mattingly is professor of history at New York University and director of NYU's *program in public history.*

The Hanging Suburbs

Hannia Gómez

Al monte, ciudadanos!
Toda acuda, toda, hacia el monte la ciudad!
(To the mountain, citizens!
All come, all, the city to the mountain!)
"Apoteosis de Bolívar," R. Agostini, 1842

Mesopotamian Memoirs

Filon of Bizantium, in his *Treaty of the Seven Wonders*, described
with surprising luxury of detail what he considered the first of
these wonders, the Hanging Gardens in the fortress of the city
of Babylon:

> The so-called Hanging Garden, having all its plants sus-
> pended, is cultivated in the air, with the roots of the trees up,
> covering as a roof the land of labor. Stone columns stand
> below and all the space on the ground is occupied by pillars.
> Trees of broad leafs and those preferred in gardens, flowers
> of all kinds and colors and, in a word, all that is merrier to
> the sight and more pleasant to enjoy grows there.... A
> caprice of art, luxurious and regal, and almost completely
> compelled by the hard work of cultivating plants hanging
> over the head of the spectators.[1]

Babylon, King Hammurabi's capital, a walled, rectangular city
form, divided in two unequal parts by the Euphrates River and
having "all the buildings within the inner wall... laid out in a

*Informal hanging suburbia. The barrios clinging from the hills reproduce by chance
the regular street-pattern of the colonial grid.*

strictly geometrical pattern with streets that were straight and of uniform width, and walls that intersected at right angles,"[2] lives more in the remembrance of its lustful suspended gardens than in any of its other urban elements. Neither the Ziggurat nor the fabulous Temple of Ishtar has transcended time like this fragment of the fortress facing the river. It is the most remembered vegetal cross-section in history.

No one can predict the paths on which cultural collective memories decide to wander. Caracas, the capital of Venezuela and a less than five-century-old Latin American city, might have more in common with ancient Babylon than do Ur, Hafaga, Arbela, Nineveh, or Khorsabad. Caracas is like Babylon not only in being organized by an orthogonal plan, being split by a river, and being virtually "walled" within the mountains, but also in manifesting wild contemporary growth on the apparently infinite hills of the south, fiercely adopting the pattern of the "Hanging Garden," a collective Mesopotamian reverie that is pending, weightless—a non-city dream. The overpopulated Hanging Suburbs are actually forcing the abandonment of central Caracas in order to foster their own capricious construction. They grow daily on steep territories, alluringly disguised as belvederes suspended over the landscape of the city they despise.

Edenic Renaissances

From the earliest times, travelers, painters, musicians, poets, and "those who know how to see, have sensed, for joy or torment, the strange fascination of the Avila,"[3] the northernmost peak of the Andes that frames the city of Caracas. Those who visit it, even just once, perceive it as one of the most beautiful places on Earth, with a tremendous tellurian power. Seduced, they call it "the Avila's spell."[4] When the Spaniards climbed the slope that brought them from the sea, seeking to make a new foundation, they were surprised at the panorama of a particularly ideal site that seemed almost to claim the birth of a city "that the mountain had been thinking with millenary tenderness."[5] Their settlement, based on the reticular pattern ordered by the Laws of Indies, gave form and meaning to the natural arcadia's urban appropriateness. Only the recent amnesia of the laws that made possible that first Caracas threatens this equilibrium.

Governor Juan of Pimentel wrote on the margin of the city's first plan of 1578, with particularly strong calligraphy, the most paradigmatic phrase in all the city's history: "and in this manner the whole town goes on being built."[6] Yet Caracas forgot how to grow. Poets sang to the intelligent and harmonious agreement they saw between the city and the landscape, but the rules to urbanize the natural landmarks of Caracas no longer count. The city's memory has disappeared. The natural landscape alone, simply because of its undeniable strength, today still manages to generate "urban forms" for Caracas—shallow forms, because the traditional city only worked linked to its immanent landscape, and the only thing contemporary Caraquenians cannot tear down completely with their bulldozers, no matter how hard they try, is the landscape. But let us see how things arrived at this state.

Latin America has few architectural texts, but is rich in poetry and literature. Venezuela is no exception to this. Not surprisingly, the relationship between Caracas and the landscape was first mentioned in verse. In the poem "America," Andrés Bello (1781–1865), author, among many works, of the best Spanish Grammar that exists yet today, sang to the ancestral infatuation between the mountain and the city. After a fire that cruelly devastated the Avila one summer, Bello decided to embrace its granite mass—to include it, to anchor it to the spaces of Caracas as another monument, as the most grandiose of buildings:

> *Brillan en las cornisas y portales*
> *de un soberbio palacio mil labores*
> *y grupos mil de antorchas y fanales*
> *el resplandor de lejos reverbera*
> *en calles, plazas, domos y miradores[7]*
> (In the cornices and porches
> of a superb palace a thousand labors gleam
> and from a distance, the radiance of
> a thousand groups of lights and torches reverberates
> in streets, domes, towers, and squares)

The superb palace will always be in the city; the mountain has become urban. All other architecture, all other fabric is compared to it. It is the city's monument by antonomasia, a monument that by virtue of the poem becomes rationally classified among the urban typologies that Caracas invents. Bello dictated nothing less than a parameter to relate all nature's icons to the city. From that point on, poets that wrote of Caracas and other Venezuelan cities have followed the directions of Bello. They repeatedly refer to Caracas and its attitude over the valley and describe it in the same terms of urban inclusion of the landscape.

The grid is the city's *inquietant ètranger*: the grid jumps over stream beds and climbs by hillsides, its surreal lapses always revealing something. The buildings nestle geometrically in the canyons, in the plains, and over depressions; the villas rectangularly dematerialize over stepped gardens. The checkerboard plan is multiplied, recreated in each one the landscape's elements, tying them, domesticating them, designing them with imagination. Such a plan should have remained in Caracas's collective memory forever.

Caracas and the Avila become inseparable in the country's literary, scientific, political, and social history, and also in its urban dialectic. The Avila is "magnificent watchtower, erect, unbeaten, intrepid voice, huge dragon, king of the Andes, Caliph, father, colossal crest, mausoleum of the city, epic, legendary, mysterious coral, God, shawl of Carlos V, paternal augur and hero," while the city is "cheerful, waste of grace and laughter and sweet outrages, languid and fine, fragrant and gentile town," that is found "hidden between hills."[8] In the romance of the land of Caracas, nature is the "giant of the city's tale." The quiet but implacable order of the one and the exaggerated exuberance of the other establishes a powerful contract, giving birth to an intuitive and unique urban tradition. This intuition was at once felt again and given literary form in 1849, in a verse by the poet Abigail Lozano, titled "A Caracas" (To Caracas), where the city is seen for the first time as a

Sultana voluptuosa reclinada del Avila en el seno colosal[9]
(Voluptuous reclining sultana of the Avila in the colossal bosom)

A decade later, in 1858, another poet, H. García de Quevedo, echoes this image in his poem *"Canto"* (Chant):

THE HANGING SUBURBS

Joven arabe *(Young Arabian Waman)*, Arturo Michelena, 1889, oil on canvas
(the Caraquenian master's only painting of an odalisque)

En la falda de un monte que engalana
feraz verdura de perpetuo abril,
tendida está, cual virgen musulmana
Caracas, la gentil[10]
(In the skirt of a mountain
adorned with the feral greenery of perpetual April,
like a Muslim virgin, is tended
Caracas, the gentile)

The native Caraquenian romanticism (rooted in the poems of
Lord Byron, John Keats, Percy Shelley, and José Zorrilla y Moral)
embraced this sensuous Orientalist image. Mariano Picón
Salas, Venezuelan historian and literary critic of the 1940s,
asserted that "all the elements on which our romanticism will
touch... already appear in García de Quevedo's '*Canto*.' "[11] The
cities are sultanas or virgins, nymphs or fairies ("Naiad of the
Anauco River" is another name for Caracas)—epithets for the
playful magic, the erotic flirting, the enlightened dialogue of the
new urban condition proposed by this City of Indies, this new
renaissance utopia implanted in Eden. The literary analogies
register the first results of a native urbanism and at the same
time influence it. Today we can say that in the dawn of this
romantic poetry is written the history of the best Caraquenian
urban tradition.

Finally, a poem by J. A. Pérez Bonalde, "Vuelta a la Patria"
(Return to the Homeland, 1880), perpetuates this city/nature
relationship:

Caracas allí está, vedla tendida
a las faldas del Avila inclinado,
Odalisca rendida
a los pies del Sultán enamorado[12]
(Caracas there it is, see her lying
at the steep Avila's skirts,
Yielded odalisque
to the enamored Sultan's feet)

The line "*Caracas allí está, vedla tendida*" became the most famous
in nineteenth-century Caraquenian literature, the Caraquenian

THE HANGING SUBURBS

urban motto. The verb *tendida*, from *tender* (to tend), invites the city to rest forever lying at the feet of the Avila, like a yielding favorite, voluptuously defeated, surrendering voluntarily . . . and mutually. *Tender* in this case evokes a romantic prostration, an apparent submission to the surrounding environment. As a consequence of this poetical conjuration, the city was seen as wanting to employ all of the synonyms of "lying" along the valley as if it were a stupendous divan: she stretched out all she could, dilated in an attempt to fill each corner, expanded toward the smaller valleys, opened, displayed, lengthened from tip to tip, unfolded, turned around, slowly first, accelerating later. As if following a desire that made her want to encompass the territory with her body, the city flirted with the idea that she shined, covering the valley with her exquisite tunics, dressing the landscape with her damasks.

The future regional carpet of disperse communities in the valleys, of buildings hung on the crags like jewelry and draperies, and the chaotic Babylon of the periphery are also a byproduct of this well-known poetic image, which continues to live inside the collective Caraquenian unconscious as a palpitating archetype. It always comes back, and must return, constantly transformed. In the old exotic metaphor, "tradition and future dialogue."[13] It does not matter that the past half century has been marked by erroneous growth: it will keep speaking of the beautiful woman that Caracas once was, of her superb natural palace, and of their intelligent urban pact.

Despite this urban mythology, the landscape began to repudiate the city, exactly when the city, detaching from itself, stopped being what it was. Around 1950 Caracas began to taste with progressive fruition new urban patterns and ideologies that were not its own. The modern urban project, in its autonomy, broke with traditional laws of growth and installed an urbanistic patchwork. Through reiterated trial and error, nature was transfigured into a kind of collective obsession. The non-changing natural environment triumphed over the unstable urban environment, always assaulted by transformation. Today most Caraquenians experience the city as "an absence, something desired but feared, a love not realized,"[14] a phenomenon recently described (again, in a literary text), by Venezuelan poet Blanca Strepponi:

A Caraquenian goes out and stops on a sidewalk....What does he see? First, the sky net, a plane of intense blue, maybe with a small cloud that only marks with its presence a beauty so perfect that it seems premeditated. What else does he see? In the northern horizon, a fragment of the splendid Avila. Something else? Yes, a smooth hill to the south, beyond Quinta Crespo; and another hill toward El Calvario, of a radiant green color with proud palm trees forming a comb in the crest. Standing in the middle of the city center's abandonment, enslaved by chaos and dirt, the Caraquenian discovers, however, when he raises his eyes up and toward the horizon, that he is surrounded by beauty. He is besieged. In the immediate ground by the unsightliness of the townscape, and in the rear ground by natural beauty.[15]

But that Caraquenian is also besieged by a third army: amnesia, because he does not remember, as nobody else does, the ideal city rooted once upon a time in this part of Eden. Therefore, for him the city is absent and has been for fifty years, when city dwellers opted to escape back to nature...not to build another city, but to enjoy the view.

Caraquenian Dreams

Caracas, like Rome, is a city of hills—not seven, but hills that, although somehow undifferentiated, in the end exist for the city to contemplate itself. The smaller of the double mountainous strings that build the valley, placed face to face to the city's great patio/*salone* and its backdrop, is in a natural way the monumental belvedere of a town that, in spite of its chaos, looks excellent at a distance. In this sense, Caracas is also like Florence. And like Florence, it has developed a recourse of urban self-viewing of very Italic derivation: the *palcoescénico*. One can simply stroll by the Florentine Fiesole, for instance, following the trails amid the hills of San Miniato and Bellosguardo, to find an array of typologies of the gaze: the Church of San Salvatore *al Monte*, Fort *Belvedere*, and the Tower of the *Observatorrio*. The Caraquenian typologies are elaborations on the same theatrical impulse to the city.

The word "*palco*" (box), which means the same in Spanish as in Italian, refers to the structure from which people view a

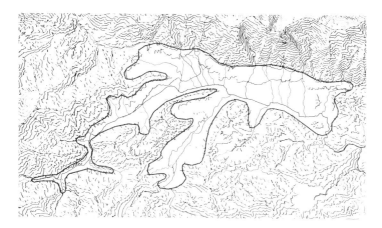

Plan of the Caracas system of valleys

The Hanging Gardens of Caracas

HANNIA GÓMEZ

spectacle, to that tiny room where few fit that hangs perilously over a theater's proscenium or over a bullring, in which the spectators struggle between the real and the visual and musical *vertigo*. As in the old operatic theaters, long and curvilinear seating, balconies, terraces, platforms, and chambers were designed to provide spectators a view of the show, and, at the same time, a place in which to be seen. This is the dream that started to be sketched on the south of Caracas during the fifties: the hills began to be urbanized in order *to look*.

For this dream to succeed, it needed a developer to demonstrate the possibility of building on the hills. The first self-proclaimed "hill-climber"[16] was Inocente Palacios, creator and planner of Colinas de Bello Monte, the inaugural Hanging Suburb of Caracas. His acrobatic urban development model, strongly anchored in the fifties aesthetics and associated with his bright Maecenasship and cultivated profile, spread all over the periphery of Caracas during the following decades. The 1950s were the golden decade of Venezuelan architecture, when the country was building its fantasies of progress. The Caraquenian dream began with that of a single Caraquenian: the lyric delirium of a developer impresario.

The suburban magnetism of Caracas starts with the singular story of Inocente Palacios's life. His constant migration to the east of downtown—from a noble paternal residence in the colonial grid, to a bigger house allowing a carport in La Candelaria, and then to a watchtower in Bello Monte—imitates the city's evolution. Palacios was born in 1908 and was a distant relative of South American liberator Simón Bolívar and of Ezequiel Zamora, leader of the Federal Revolution. This heritage conferred upon him a certain halo of patrician rebellion that was very useful for him in many ways. As a revolutionary youth, Palacios belonged to the intellectual Generation of '28, which opposed the military dictatorship of the twenties. Later, he dedicated his life to the visual arts, music, and, lastly, to urbanism, where, literally, he opened new roads. Yet he ended up as a cultural entrepreneur and a pioneer of art education. He founded the School of Arts of the Central University of Venezuela in 1978, as well as several music schools, and served as Venezuelan commissary at international art biennials and organizer of the

Caracas Music Festival during the 1950s.[17] Upon his death in 1996, the press called him one of "the illustrious men that will always give pride to Venezuela."[18]

In the history of the architecture and urbanism of Caracas, Inocente Palacios's results are legendary. His musical passion, along with his close connection to Brazilian architecture through his friendship with Oscar Niemeyer, shaped his urban vision as well as his urban ambition. He said,

> When Brasilia was being finished, Oscar Niemeyer invited me to witness it. That city was built by a human flock that lived on the slopes. When it began to live, it turned out to be a fictitious entity, false, placed in the middle of that other turbulent city that is the Brasilia of the ones who built it. Its own life is on the hillsides: what was built by those carpenters, masons, bricklayers, and later intellectuals, writers, and journalists. The great city is the slopes: there the future Brasilia was formed.[19]

Palacios's romanticism for the urban life "on the slopes" together with the impact produced on him by Niemeyer's house formed the model of Bello Monte. According to Palacios, Niemeyer is a cliff *aficionado*:

> He doesn't live in the city, he lives in the country. But far in the country, on an extraordinary site, a big bay of the sea; and at the summit of a great incline, in that shell that is thus formed, with mountains behind, is, as a live corpuscle, the house of Oscar. A very small house, with all nature inserted within, a marvel.[20]

Palacios began to be openly devoted to urbanism, and became a cultural developer playing urban developer. Assisted by Italian architect Antonio Lombardini, called the "architect of *colinas*," and a team of the best architects and engineers, he created Colinas de Bello Monte. It would have been impossible for him not to be driven by the theatrical analogy he was offered by the land. He justified development in the hills by saying, "In those years people thought that Caracas needed to grow because the valley was getting too small."[21] But such an escalation of development was not really so urgent in the half-empty Caracas of the 1950s; it was clearly an act of urbanistic illusion of the spreading city apparently filling up the valley.

People were coerced into moving upwards to the hills, a phenomenon that began with an innovative real-estate marketing idea: let's sell the tickets of the theater's seats. In parallel, the informal city of the *barrios* began on the other side of the vertical periphery. Bello Monte, even in its name, is sold like an ideal place. In a promotional poster, the image of the hills appears as superimposed color waves that could easily be taken for a musical score—a Verdi opera, lyric papers of a singing club, topographic lines of a perpendicular Arcadia, a *sviluppo residenziale* where a good view was guaranteed without opposing the original mount's topographical and landscaping harmony.

The toponymic vicinity of Bello Monte to the Italian places of Mount Posillipo, Montecassino, Montecatini, or Monticello inspires us to imagine the hill planners performing their building epic with orchestrated bulldozers, and engineers with batons, to the musical and operatic monumentality. With a layout half organic, half totalitarian, the streets merge with the labyrinth. In the past remains the clarity of the grid. Its intricate web always cheats on you, loyal to topography but also listening to signs coming from the city in front of it. The dangerously stressed slopes are unavoidable challenges to engineering skills, something very typical of the decade. The emphasis is first to make the visitor lost, then surprise him at a curve's turn with the discovery sometimes of a fantastic panorama, sometimes of the perplexing architecture *de época*. An architecture "of specialists," as it is known enigmatically, is still today among the most frantically formalistic in the city.

The 1950s were the decade of European, especially Mediterranean, immigration to Venezuela, initiated by the country's economic bonanza. The major works of the period, the City University, the Simón Bolívar Center, the highways and other works of engineering, and, of course, the urban plans, employed a large number of men newly immigrated from countries of great constructive tradition. These are the "specialists," fugitives of the political and economic problems of their homelands. Architects, engineers, and artisans of all kinds arrived to fill the country with the architectural and urban traces of their remembrances.[22] The "developer impresario" employed these people to elaborate the emblematic Belmontine typologies. Lombardini designed for him Caurimare, a house/conservatory standing "on one of those peaks,"[23] a house so big, so "absurdly big we held many grandiose concerts, at times even with up to forty musicians."[24] Niemeyer drew for him the preliminary project of an art museum for Caracas, an inverted pyramid resting on the edge of a ravine, absurdly stable on its minimal vertex.

Palacios also sponsored and built in a glen the Acoustic Shell, "an open-air stage of extraordinary facilities and excellent acoustics,"[25] to celebrate his musical festivals; he called for an international competition to design a house prototype for Bello Monte, whose main requirement was that it could hold onto the most acute slope. The winning project, a small prototype "set like an eagle's nest on a rock,"[26] was premiered with festive air "to demonstrate it could be done."[27] Thus "fabulous things in Colinas,"[28] dramatic villas in cantilever, were incubated and appeared with echoes from Carlo Scarpa and Adalberto Libera, "those houses that appeared hanging."[29] Palacios was also the mentor of daring architectural projects that he commissioned to the best architects: Fruto Vivas made his iconic hyperbolic paraboloid of the Club Táchira; Jimmy Alcock the undulating brick ribbon of the Altolar Building; Martin Vegas & Jose Miguel Galia their legendary twin buildings.

The optic adventure of the Bello Monte suburb is composed of rationalist lyricisms hung on the abyss, cantilevered *gesti di ingenieri*, level curves shaped in concave and convex harmonies by the millimeter, vedute and nomenclature full of Messalinas, Michelangelos, Tiberiuses, Cesars, Neros, and Fontane d'Amore. Its urbanistic plan is as scientifically visual as Milan's La Scala, while its architecture embarks on a formal search as heretic as that of modern architecture in postwar Italy. This suburban ideal slices in steps the bucolic hills and their *piemonte*, yet has no communal services, no sidewalks, and no urban public space, proving how far a developer can spread his personal obsessions into other people's lives.[30] The obsession, the Florentine dream of a single Caraquenian, became collective. With it came the valley's abandonment, the escape from order, and the amnesia of the old ideal of the city.

Caracas is Caracas and the Rest is Weeds and Snakes

City and Caraquenian suburbs compete at all costs to be called "Caracas." But neither exist psychologically as such: while the city is sadly removed from its own and universal urban culture and memory, its suburbs do not want to recognize themselves as the periphery—they want to be *the city*. We find ourselves before the curious cases of a non-city and a non-suburbia, questioning whether the suburbs will continue to exist.[31] This confusing center/periphery dialectic does not want to be straightforwardly performed.

But, as in other places, the "structuralist reading" that speaks of the city "as a dominant center and a dependent periphery"[32] is becoming progressively illegible. When we observe many of the global phenomena of the "once binary"[33] metropolis, we see that the monocentric city is eroding (the center of Caracas is a filthy ruin) and fragmenting into the polycentric metropolis (the boroughs of Chacao, Petare, Baruta, and El Hatillo, all peripheral governments, have almost as much political voice as the municipality of Caracas.

Likewise, nature is being transformed into a pseudo-city of "marginal discourse" (the greenbelt is being supplanted). Forty years ago, a school of planners that had inherited its theories and methods from the English modern experience approached the problem of growth in Caracas by devising a protective zone, based on "other greenbelts like the Greater London Plan of [Sir Patrick] Abercrombie's team and Amsterdam's master plan."[34] They froze undeveloped territory to guarantee the city a dose of nature, coined a green label with the initials PZ (protective zone), and painted it on the Caracas plan along an irregular semicircle between Catia and Guarenas. Nothing was to be erected there; all was to be left to the tropical jungle.

This zoning was never sufficiently established to protect the natural environment, as occurs, for example, with the decrees that determine the limits in a national park. Caracas's greenbelt was an unqualified "rear setback," a city's backyard, a void reserved (tacitly) for future growth of the urban area while it was being decided how that growth would come, a lot for expansions. Thus outlined, it succumbed very quickly to the Caraquenian vices of all setbacks: immediate violation, irrational construction, and consequent anarchic suburbanization.

Besides, from the start zoning ordinances for the development on the hills absurdly permitted a very high building-to-ground-area ratio, figures more typical of an urban center, contradicting the protective policy. As a result, buildings of twenty and more stories high were constructed in the most absurd places. Planning laws exist, but nobody knows exactly for what—if for favoring the countryside, the city, or neither.

A situation so ambiguous could not help but attract the pleasure of evasion, the skillful breaking of laws. The greenbelt of the Caracas metropolitan area became a field of battles. Urban and peasant invasions, residential complexes, clubs and villas, and even floating islands that look like city centers were attractive, licensable, and possible to build. Notwithstanding the unstable condition of most of the steep lands and a tendency for disastrous landslides, the Caracas suburbs, high-class clusters or *barrios*, continue hanging wildly.[35]

Ignorance of regional geology and warnings against development[36] did not stop the bulldozers, the deforestation, and the illegal exploitation of quarries. Due to the unexplainable absence of a planning authority today, the plans of the governmental office in charge during the era of development, the Ministry of Public Works, have been maintained by inertia. Their understanding of the suburban reality is so ridiculously abstract that their colored-spot plans are derisively known as "MOP art."

Eighty percent of the Venezuelan population is urban, and of that number, the majority lives at the periphery of cities. Contemporary Caraquenians share as a common feature their "resistance to being citizens, the difficulty of perceiving themselves as such, and hostility, in its broadest sense."[36] Most of them do not know about the quiet suburban war where the key struggles for the future of the city are being fought: the form of the city versus the landscape's integrity, the survival of the ecosystem versus the need to grow, the endowment of services versus accessibility, the monocentric city versus the independent communities, investment in the periphery versus the center's erosion, experimentation versus memory, fragmentation versus urban continuity, to see versus to be seen.

These suburbanites live in a state of perennial and romantic unidirectional observation of Caracas that keeps their sight clouded, "nomads creating and recreating their own fiction of the city."[37] Their Caracas only exists to be seen from the south of the Guaire River, only deserves to be envisaged with a mountain as a backdrop. It is logical, then, for them to consider that everything behind their backs is weeds and snakes, or, at best, a backyard. Amid this absence, amid this confusion, all that remains is the landscape's force. Its lustful vegetation conceals the city as well as the suburbs; branches erase their edges, tree tops soften their angles, flowers swallow their blunders. Architectural profiles and urban features are blurred, but it does not matter much: the backdrop city, the panorama city, the distant city still looks good from afar; its faint urban memory is also at a distance. Everything disappears amid the green.

The neglectfulness with which the southern hills and valleys of Caracas have been urbanized is but a direct reflex of this voyeuristic pose. Only if suburbanites are forced to stare at the townscape in the opposite direction, that is, from north to south (an unnatural position for any Caraquenian), will they face the pathetic exploding chaos of all the formal and informal growth.

Caracas, there it is: vertical and intricate, for half a century built in the shade, outside any functional, structural, formal, or landscaping concern. And, although it is something Caraquenians hate to accept, the contemporary image of the city is now that of the Hanging Suburbs, that "having all its plan[t]s suspended, is cultivated in the air.[38]

1. Filon of Bizantium, *Tratado de las Siete Maravillas* (Treaty of the Seven Wonders) I, cited in Juan Antonio Ramírez, *Construcciones ilusorias: arquitecturas descritas, arquitecturas pintadas* (Illusory Constructions: Described Architectures, Painted Architectures) (Madrid: Alianza Editorial, S.A., 1983), 249–50.
2. Leonardo Benévolo, *The History of the City* (Cambridge, MA: MIT Press, 1980), 28–33.
3. Angel Rafael Insausti, "El Avila en el verso" (The Avila in the Verse), in *Revista Shell*, vol. 5, no. 18 (March 1956): 36–43.
4. Ibid., 37.
5. Ibid., 36.
6. Juan de Pimentel, "Primer Plano de Santiago de León de Caracas, 1578" (First Plan of Santiago de León de Caracas, 1578), in Irma de Sola-Ricardo, *Contribución al Estudio de los Planos de Caracas, La ciudad y la Provincia, 1567–1967* (Contribution to the Study of the Plans of Caracas, The City and the Province, 1567–1967) (Caracas: Ediciones del Cuatricentenario de Caracas, 1967), 30.
7. Andrés Bello, "America" (1823), cited in Insausti, "El Avila," 38.
8. Insausti, "El Avila," 39.
9. Abigail Lozano, "A Caracas" (1849), cited in ibid., 40.

10. H. García de Quevedo, "Canto" (1858), cited in Insausti, "El Avila," 40.

11. Mariano Picón Salas, *Formación y proceso de la literatura venezolana* (Formation and Process of Venezuelan Literature) (Caracas: Asociación de Escritores de Venezuela, 1940), 145.

12. J. A. Pérez Bonalde, "Vuelta a la Patria" (1880), cited in Insausti, "El Avila," 41.

13. Insausti, "El Avila," 43.

14. Blanca Strepponi, "Nuestra naturaleza es mental" (Our Nature is Mental), lecture from the forum "Atmósferas Urbanas" (Urban Atmospheres) Banco Unión, Caracas, 1996; printed in *El Nacional's Literary Paper* (Caracas), 28 July 1996, 1.

15. Ibid.

16. Inocente Palacios, cited in Hannia Gómez and William Niño Araque, *Fragmentos de una entrevista a Inocente Palacios* (Fragments from an Interview with Inocente Palacios), unpublished document, 1989, 3.

17. Zayira Arenas, "Con Inocente Palacios se va una Venezuela exceptional" (With Inocente Palacios Ends an Exceptional Venezuela), *El Nacional* (Caracas), 20 October 1996, C6.

18. Ibid.

19. Palacios, cited in Gómez and Araque, *Fragmentos de una entrevista*, 3.

20. Ibid.

21. Ibid.

22. Hannia Gómez, "Lunguaire," *El Diario de Caracas* (Caracas), 9 July 1995, 4.

23. Palacios, cited in Gómez and Araque, *Fragmentos de una entrevista*, 4.

24. Ibid., 5.

25. Alfredo Rugeles, "Con alma de músico" (With a Musician's Soul), *El Nacional* (Caracas), 20 October 1996, C6.

26. Palacios, cited in Gómez and Araque, *Fragmentos de una entrevista*, 5.

27. Ibid.

28. Ibid.

29. Ibid.

30. Gómez, "Lunguaire," 4.

31. Jonathan Woodroffe, Dominic Papa, and Ian McBurnie, "The Periphery—An Introduction," *Architectural Design Profile* 18 (1994): 7.

32. Ibid., 6.

33. Ibid.

34. Fernando Tábora, "La Zona Protectora: ¿Greenpeace o Greenwar?" (The Protective Zone: Greenpeace or Greenwar?), lecture presented at forum "12 Temas para Repensar la Ciudad" (12 Themes on Rethinking the City), Consolidated Cultural Center, Caracas, 14 November 1996.

35. Hannia Gómez, "Campo de Justas" (Field of Battles), *El Nacional* (Caracas), 18 November 1996, C5.

36. Strepponi, *Nuestra naturaleza es mental*, 1.

37. Woodroffe, Papa, and McBurnie, *Periphery*, 7.

38. Filon of Bizantium, *Tratado de las Siete Maravillas*, cited in Ramírez, *Construcciones ilusorias*, 249.

Hannia Gómez is a Venezuelan architect.

Dust Control (Yallambie), *Darren Wardle*

The Lucky Country: Myth, Image, and the Australian Suburb

Laurel Porcari and Peter Zellner

The late Robin Boyd, undoubtedly Australia's most eminent urban theorist and social critic, argued in the preface to *Australia's Home*, his groundbreaking critique of the Australian domestic building, that "the small house, probably more than anything else that man has done, has made the face of Australia and to an extent the faces of Australians."[1] When Boyd penned those words forty-five years ago, Australia—like America in the early fifties—was entering an era of rapid urban expansion and social change. In the forty years following the Second World War, Australia's cities nearly doubled in size. Around Australia's three major urban conglomerations (Sydney, Melbourne, and Brisbane) new suburban developments swallowed the old colonial city centers whole. Immigrants and refugees from Europe and Asia flocked to the antipodes in search of a new life, swelling the nation's population by twenty-five percent and changing the face of Australian culture as they introduced different customs to Australia's Anglo-Celtic heartlands. Inevitably, Australia was moving away from its pastoral, agrarian beginnings towards a manufacturing-, service-, and information-based economy. By 1995, almost three-quarters of the Australian urban population was living in suburban areas, making Australians some of the most suburbanized people on the planet.[2]

In Australia, homeownership and suburban sprawl are readily equated with the good life and prosperity. When Australia was first christened "the lucky country," Australians pointed to its status as the first "suburban nation" as proof of its standing in the world. Yet despite these facts, Australia has often clung to its colonial and pastoral history and rural icons (such as the infamous highwayman, underdog, and national hero Ned Kelly and Australia's unofficial national anthem *Waltzing Matilda*) when depicting itself to the outside or defining itself within national debates. The images and legends Australia repeatedly selects to describe itself are usually of the bush or colonial variety (a young country setting itself up in the wilds of a new world) or more recently of the sun- and surf-drenched tourist destination sort (the ideal place to get away from the pressures of the "real world"). As Boyd noted,

> A century after the goldrush, the lean, tanned Australian of the outback, creasing his eyes against the sun, was one of the stock characters of the world. The surfer, the life-saver parading at Manly, the wide white beach packed with sunbathers eating ham sandwiches—these were the Australians of the newsreel and travel brochure.[3]

These motifs continue to inform the manner in which Australia chooses to engage the world through its mediated image: as the last great untamed continent or a southern paradise. The Australia of recent films, of *Priscilla, Queen of the Desert*, of *The Man From Snowy River*, or of *Crocodile Dundee*, is an Australia unfettered by suburban sprawl, racial conflict, freeway jams, and "Coca-Colonization." Australia also puts forth its Aboriginal identity (witness the recent Olympic images of Sydney with its kangaroo bicyclists and token Aboriginal dancers) while the nation's suburban culture remains largely a caricature (as depicted by the popular television soap operas "Neighbours" and "Home and Away").

However, it is not our intention here to criticize the development of Australia's world image or to draw any more attention to the apparent conflict existing between that image and the nation's suburban realities. Rather, we wish to trace how Australia's physical (suburban) and imagined (mythologized) conditions are inextricably linked and have paradoxically developed in support of each other.

The formation of the Australian suburb and the development of Australian national ideologies and iconographies occurred, not coincidentally, at about the same time—around the close of the nineteenth century. From their moment of inception, Australia's colonial capitals were developed around a suburban framework, and indeed by the late 1800s those capitals were predominantly suburban in arrangement. As the historian Graeme Davison has pointed out,

> The suburban idea arrived with the country's European founders and it was vigorously promoted by the state during the early colonial period. . . . It had a strong appeal to immigrants who were themselves largely refugees from urban Britain. Australia may be thought of as the farthest suburb of Britain and ambitions for land, space, and independence frustrated in the crowded cities of the homeland were often realized on the suburban frontiers of Australia.[4]

In *Homes and Homesteads in the Land of Plenty*, a guide to Australian domesticity published in 1871, author James Ballantyne asks, second-guessing his presumably British working-class reader,

> What can [he] gain by going to Victoria? . . . He will be able, whether by economy or saving or through the help of one of the numerous building societies, to secure a comfortable freehold for himself and . . . possess what every Englishman glories in—a house which will be his castle.[5]

During the 1890s, Australia's prose and poetry writers—such as Henry Lawson and "Banjo" Patterson—were developing a national character contrary to this suburban development, based instead upon bush and pastoral imagery. These writers equated the city and its suburbs with the vileness of industrialization, materialism, and homogeneity, and sought to define Australia's national identity around the hearty virtues of the pastoral life in the bush. They championed the masculine exploits of the pioneer, the stockman, the sheepshearer, the bush ranger, and the farmer as genuine emerging national types.[6] In so doing they helped lay the foundations for Australian popular culture and by extension the character of the Australian suburb as it is experienced by the average Australian.

This nationalist rural mythology was reinforced by the work of the Heidelberg School of fine artists, which included the painters Arthur Streeton and Frederick McCubbin. Turning their backs on the city of Melbourne and the suburb of Heidelberg in which they worked, these artists literally faced towards the pastoral horizon in order to paint images of the bush that "allowed 'city bushmen' to imagine an affiliation with bush life, even if their only contact with it was through illustrated newspapers or sedate picnics at designated beauty spots."[7] Thus, while Australia's suburbs grew in response to the urges and desires of the colonial immigrant for an egalitarian existence and freedom from the enforced class differences of the old world, artists like Streeton put the suburbs behind them, at once discrediting the very existence of Australian suburbs by rendering visions of exclusivity and distance from them while simultaneously marketing their work for consumption by suburbanites. Paintings like *Near Heidelberg*, Streeton's depiction of a country paddock being traversed by day-tripping city folk in their finery, concealed, rather than explained, suburban expansion.

In defining a national ethos, the experiences of a minority, as lived in the bush, were substituted for the lives of the majority, as lived in the suburbs. This act of distancing and inversion set into motion a self-perpetuating image: the myth of the heroic bushman as interpreted from the safety of the tamed suburb. Fittingly, it was at Canberra, the nascent Australian capital and the symbolic heart of the Australian national consciousness, where this oscillating dance of distancing and inversion would be played out during the first half of the twentieth century.

Canberra, a locality about halfway between Australia's two major cities (Sydney and Melbourne) was selected as the nation's capital by the Australian Federation in 1901. An international design competition was announced in 1911 to search for a design scheme that would embody the young country's aspirations. The competition was won in 1912 by two American architects, Walter Burley Griffin and Marion Mahoney Griffin, both of whom were disciples of Frank Lloyd Wright. Their experiences working in and around Chicago during the ascension of the Prairie School and their exposure to the architecture and planning work of Daniel H. Burnham and John Wellborn Root greatly influenced their attitudes towards nature and urbanity.

Those attitudes were manifest in the Griffins' design for Canberra. The scheme symbolized the unity of the newly formed federation's democratic identity. It was a vision of a political utopia that exerted power on behalf of all for the greater good. It manipulated the Australian landscape, using nature in a monumental fashion—as an equal to architecture. Towards this end, it used the landscape "as a container and as a primary repository of symbolic meaning."[8] The Griffin plan drew legible relationships between all parts of the capital city and the city's natural surroundings. Within the plan, a grand ceremonial land axis and a parliamentary triangle were linked to the adjacent commercial and residential districts. In their vision for a national capital, the Griffins proposed the construction of an epic landscape that would at once embody the nationalist myths of the rural experience and Australia's egalitarian culture. They did not set out to simulate the raw and the wild, but to form associations between nature and Australia's national vision of itself. Prophetically, Canberra would be nicknamed the "bush capital" and the "natural capital."

Australia's capital, having been set back by bureaucratic meddling, two world wars, and the Depression, was not completed until 1958. As it was constructed, the relationship between Canberra's ceremonial land axis, the parliamentary triangle, the adjacent commercial and residential nodes, and the natural surroundings was unclear. Sadly, much of the Griffins' vision was lost in a wash of developer-style cul-de-sac suburban allotments. What was conceived of in 1912 as a landscaped city had degenerated into a city as suburban landscape. Unlike the magnificent, untamed bush and expansive outback to which the capital aspired, Canberra was realized as a totally synthetic environment—a planned suburban capital of loosely knitted precincts connected by gently curving roads with generous shoulders and large nebulous buffer zones of manicured native foliage.[9] Tragically, the Griffins' vision for an Arcadian city was transformed by the introduction of the car, the road, and the backyard—the "holy triumvirate" of twentieth-century suburban living.

At mid-century, the Australian suburb underwent a period of unprecedented mutation and dramatic expansion that mirrored Australia's postwar modernization and industrialization programs and the nation's entry into the global consumer and media economies. The massive demand for new homes during the fifties stemmed from both the needs of the expanding

Australian middle class and the waves of newly enfranchised immigrants. Rapid and unchecked development of new suburbs satisfied both the practical needs of a nation engaged in its own baby boom and the moral imperatives of a culture determined to participate in the politic of a new world order. As Sir Robert Menzies, one of Australia's longest-serving prime ministers, augured during a radio broadcast delivered three years before the close of the Second World War,

> The material home represents the concrete expression of the habits of frugality and saving "for a home of your own." Your advanced socialist may rage against private property even whilst he acquires it; but one of the best instincts in us is that which induces us to have one little piece of earth with a house and a garden which is ours. . . . My home is where my wife and children are; the instinct to be with them is the instinct of civilized man.[10]

By Menzies's estimation the home (and not the farm) had become the bastion of Australian society. Homeownership was equated with moral rectitude, national pride, and, by extension, the rhetoric of international, capitalist modernization.

The suburban growth that Australia embraced as the new national ethos threatened to dilute the essential, mythical Australian identity, leading Boyd to lament,

> What has happened to the spirit, the gusto, the faith? The twentieth century seems to have tamed and deadened the Australian character. . . . The Wild Colonial Boy is selling used cars.[11]

The home, household goods, and the family car had won out over the legends of the bush. The political and governmental creation of a new suburban imperative firmly fixed Australians within the global economy of mass advertising and consumption.

Oddly, the "cultural void" created by the new suburbs seemed to revitalize the regional identity that Boyd mourned. Though the triumph of American-styled consumerism in Australia's new ring-suburbs marked the loss of a genuine national character, the benefits these suburbs delivered to new-home buyers perversely reinvented the myths constructed around the bush for space-age consumption. As art historian

Chris McAulliffe notes in *Art and Suburbia,* "The large numbers of Australians who economized by building their own homes generated a popular image of the suburban owner-builder as the new pioneer."[12] The quarter-acre block of land and the free-standing dwelling promised by the fifties dream of homeowner-ship offered average Australians the opportunity to engage and sustain the national myths that Streeton and his colleagues had striven so hard to perpetuate some sixty years earlier. With a backyard paddock to run the animals (dogs) and a barbecue pit to "gather the clan around," every ranch-style home in the sub-urbs delivered, in miniature, a chance for "everyman" to live like a rugged outdoorsman.

In addition, the new technologies of the car and the trailer facilitated a paradoxical reengagement with the romantic vision of pioneering settlers crossing the great open untamed spaces of the new world. The late-model car parked alongside the house and the sleek mobile home or trailer that inevitably accompanied it provided Australians with newly acquired levels of mobility and freedom. Families unaccustomed to traveling further than the next suburb suddenly set off on extended interstate vacations. For suburbanites who experienced the bush from the comfort of a Holden or Ford family sedan, the caravan park (replete with its dwarflike urban infrastructures, carefully land-scaped and contoured roadways, and condensed allotments) must have seemed altogether normal.

While Australia's suburbs densify and encroach, the desire for the expansive and free existence depicted in the visions of the Heidelberg School is improbably accelerated and intensified by the contemporary Australian media. Current popular television shows like "Burke's Backyard," a gardening program, and "Healthy, Wealthy and Wise," a life-style program, continue to proffer the image of Australia as a rustic, nonsuburban nation. Television advertisers hitch the suburbanite's acquisitiveness to the mythologies of the bush in order to sell Australians every-thing from cars to cosmetics. Television ads aimed at affluent Australians depict young urban professionals racing across the outback in the latest-model four-wheel-drive Holden Jackeroo ("jackeroo" is the colloquial term for a farm or station hand), attired in "authentic" Australian apparel by Country Road or

R. M. Williams, and shielded from the fierce elements by Red Earth cosmetics. Apparently it does not matter if the all-terrain vehicle is really used to drive to the supermarket or if the genuine bush clothing are modeled after those in *The Man from Snowy River.*

Today, it is no longer necessary to make a physical connection between the suburb and the originating heroic mythologies of the bush. The relationship is now visual or, more likely, virtual. Televisual culture supplies a surrogate connection to the myths of the bush. The contemporary Australian suburbanite, the everyman, identifies with the image of someone else connecting with the landscape. The free-spirited colonist whose tamed nature Boyd lamented in the fifties is no longer even selling used cars: he has been reduced to a marketing device.

The quintessentially modern culture of the car and TV and the romantic vision of life in nineteenth-century Australia initiated a strange alliance in the Australian suburb of the fifties. This alliance anticipated the compression of the egalitarian culture of the city and the rural ethos of the outback into a single media entity during the last quarter of this century. These urban and rural cultures, intersecting in the suburbs through the real technologies of the roadway and the virtual technologies of the digital and televisual revolution, formed a condition of super-adjacency and transparency, a hyper-proximity of image/symbol and experience stretching thinly across the roadside billboard or floating freely in the ether of the televised spectacle.

Australia's defining national image, free from the constraints of urban reality, has become pure, transparent, and unadulterated. *Dust Control (Yallambie)*, a recent painting by Melbourne artist Darren Wardle, effectively describes this image as it has arrived in contemporary Heidelberg (see frontispiece).[13] In Wardle's painting of a new subdivision, a copy of Albrecht Dürer's *The Young Hare* floats in front of a manicured housing estate. In the lower left corner of the canvas, the artist has painted himself gazing over the estate through a pair of binoculars. The central overlaid image refers to the ubiquitous nature of the nonindigenous, colonizing rabbit (and the warren-like, ceaselessly repetitive suburb), while Wardle's portrayal of himself symbolizes the modern suburban dweller, a contemporary voyeur scanning the urban environment in front of him. It is telling that Wardle's binoculars are aimed at a billboard in front of a new subdivision, named—not unknowingly— "Streeton Views." Here, Streeton's aspiration to create a genuine national identity found in the heroic exploits of the bush, and not in the "base" values of the egalitarian suburb, is reduced to a one-liner, an advertising jingle.

Amazingly, the mechanisms of desire, as manufactured by the developer and the television programmer, have compacted the conflicting grand narratives of the Australian experience onto the flattened surface of the roadside signboard and the TV screen. The Australian suburb, no longer able to effectively hold or contain these competing national histories, has become televisual rather than picturesque.

1. Robin Boyd, *Australia's Home* (Melbourne: Penguin Books, 1978), preface.
2. According to the 1991 census, Australian Bureau of Statistics, 71.1% of Australians living in cities of more than 100,000 people inhabited suburban areas.
3. Boyd, *Australia's Home*, 228.
4. Graeme Davison, "The Past and the Future of the Australian Suburb," *Polis* vol. 1, no. 1 (February 1994): 5.
5. James Ballantyne, *Homes and Homesteads in the Land of Plenty* (Melbourne: Mason, Firth and M'Cutcheon, 1871).
6. For further discussion of this phenomenon see Harriet Edquist, "The Landscape of Desire," *B Architectural Magazine* 52/53 (1996): 86–87 and Chris McAulliffe, *Art and Suburbia* (Sydney: Craftsman House, 1996).
7. McAulliffe, *Art and Suburbia*, 46.
8. Christopher Vernon, "Canberra and the Persistence of Landscape," *B Architectural Magazine* 52/53 (1996): 36.
9. Ibid., 33.
10. Menzies delivered this statement in 1942 as part of a radio broadcast entitled "The Forgotten People" At the time he was the Australian Parliamentary Opposition leader.
11. Boyd, *Australia's Home*, 295.
12. McAulliffe, *Art and Suburbia*, 67.
13. Yallambie, a suburb of Melbourne, is named after Allambie, a mishearing of *ngaiambi*, which means "to remain, to dwell" in Woiwurrung (the dialect used by Aborigines living south of the Great Dividing Range). Sally Steward, ed., *Australian Phrasebook* (Melbourne: Lonely Planet Publications, 1994), 157.

Laurel Porcari is an architect, urban designer, and lecturer in the Department of Architecture at RMIT University.

Peter Zellner is an architect and lecturer in the Faculty of Environmental Design and Construction at RMIT University.

The Aesthetics of Unsightliness

Christoph Allenspach

photographs by Jules Spinatsch

Using inexpensive materials but a great deal of time, European star architects have built a city that meets the future: Euralille, the new European transit junction on the outskirts of the French city Lille. The new traffic and transportation center is supposed to improve the economy of northern France and support and stimulate the business relations and the exchange between distinguished European cities.

In the 1970s, the economy of Lille, based mostly on the coal, steel, and textile industries, had collapsed. After this breakdown, the idea of a Euro Tunnel offered a new economical chance for Lille, which is located between the major European cities of Brussels, London, Paris, Amsterdam, and Cologne. Lille's ambitious mayor, Pierre Mauroy, a former member of François Mitterrand's government, realized the opportunity for Lille to become a transit center located at the entrance of the Euro Tunnel. It was because of him that the "Eurostar"—the new European super train—was detoured to Lille.

In 1987 Jean-Paul Baïetto, an experienced urban planner and former director of the French State Department of Planning, was hired to coordinate the mega project. Baïetto's approach is to build only what is reasonable for the market. His performance in Lille is more than remarkable: in less than seven years the first 173 acres were built up.

Euralille train station

Triangle des gares, Jean Nouvel

Interior of Triangle des gares

THE AESTHETICS OF UNSIGHTLINESS

Grand Palais, Rem Koolhaas

Lobby of Grand Palais

Euralille world trade center; at left is "L" Tower, Christian de Portzamparc

A jury selected designs by Rem Koolhaas (Grand Palais), Jean Nouvel (Triangle des gares), Christian de Portzamparc ("L" Tower), and Claude Vasconi (Lille Europe). These parts of the project, which are built for the region, are working successfully, but other parts intended for wider European use are still dead. The new station, designed for the French high-speed TGV train and the new European super train "Eurostar," was predicted to serve at least 15,000 passengers a day. In early 1996, only five trains a day were leaving for London, four trains for Paris, and three for Brussels, together less than half of the scheduled departures.

Originally published in Facts *vol. 6 no. 8 (February 1996).*
(Translated from the German by Andrea Nussbaum)

Christoph Allenspach is a German journalist.

Jules Spinatsch is a Swiss photographer.

THE AESTHETICS OF UNSIGHTLINESS

Lille and Euralille

Nanni Moretti in Caro Diario *(Dear Diary, 1993)*

Ambiguous Sovereignties: Notes on the Suburbs in Italian Cinema

Giorgio Bertellini and Saverio Giovacchini

—What would be great is a film just of houses: panning shots of houses: Garbatella, 1927; Villaggio Olimpico, 1960; Tufello, 1960; Vigne Nuove, 1987; Monteverde, 1939 . . .
—Excuse me. Why did you move to Casalpalocco?
—The green, this peace . . .
—Yeah, green. . . . You moved here around 1961?
—In '62.
—Thirty years ago, Rome was a marvelous city!
—It's different here.
—But Rome was beautiful, then!
            Nanni Moretti, *Caro Diario* (Dear Diary, 1993)

Rome: Exterior Day
A summer afternoon in the early 1990s. Director Nanni Moretti wanders around the capital riding his scooter. Following him, the camera tracks along the streets, crossroads, and corners of the city brightened by the Mediterranean sunlight. Nobody is around; all the theaters are closed because of the traditional summer break, with the exception of porno establishments and a few others showing the asphyxiating and agoraphobic Italian films of the decade. From his Vespa, Moretti praises a cinema capable of showing the various facades of the city's buildings, both urban and suburban, with their different architectural and

historical configurations, and screams his utter love for work-ing-class districts and houses—only to confess finally his pref-erence for those fancy and costly lofts that he cannot afford.

Through these few images and lines, Moretti touches upon Italian urban and cinematic history, and upon the political and intellectual dilemma of a leftist figure caught between the pub-lic obligation of populist solidarity and the private search for elit-ist comfort. As a result, what at first sight may appear as a lim-ited pursuit of the cinematic rendering of the cityscape brings into question broader, long-standing debates about class, ideol-ogy, and the urban territory.

An investigation of the poetic tensions between cinema and suburbia, in fact, raises crucial questions. What is the ideologi-cal space for the emergence in Italy of a cinematic discourse about the cityscape? If suburbia is to be understood as the social, architectural, and cultural body located over and outside the city's edge, how did it develop, not only historically but also con-ceptually, as the "suburban discourse"? Who lives in it, and who does not? From which point of view is the "suburban scene" observed and constructed? Finally, is Italian cinematic suburbia something more than a mere spatial trope that intrinsically opposes center/periphery, inside/outside, inclusion/exclusion? In our opinion, the suburban discourse is a heavily charged political event, where the rescue and the invention of working-class traditions, national identity, and democratic participation play a primary role.

The Invention of the National Masses and their New Locations

At the turn of the century the problem of low-rent housing developed in Italy as a question regarding the daily lives of new social formations. As early as 1903, the first Giovanni Giolitti government enacted measures to meet the mounting need for cheap domiciles. Yet, the rising cost of living, the process of urbanization, the housing shortage, and the increasing number of slums and blighted areas confronted the housing agencies throughout the following decades.[1] In addition, the end of the Great War marked a deep housing crisis. On 30 November 1919 the postwar Italian government promulgated a law to coordinate all previous legislation about housing matters, which later inspired and informed the Fascist regime's housing policies. During the interwar years, the regime's urban policy, in fact, tended to correlate housing distribution with class origins. Thus, such policies erased Italy's historical, interclass neighborhoods. In the name of urban regeneration (*risanamento*), municipal planning created outer, often isolated, low-rent zones, and carefully distinguished among building types such as the engineer's house (*casa dell'ingegnere*), the functionary's house (*casa dell'impiegato*), the worker's house (*casa dell'operaio*), and the rural house (*casa rurale*).[2]

While Fascist urban planning from the mid-1920s consistently created new isolated neighborhoods throughout Italy—in Rome these public project areas were called *borgate*—the "cinema under Fascism" devoted little attention to the everyday struggles of low-income tenants living in those new suburban enclaves. Generally speaking, the realist codes of the Italian film productions of the 1930s displayed the tone of a paternalistic, manipulative, possession of the masses, either in the name of Italy's glorious past and its popular heroes, or in the name of a newly nationalized rural tradition, depository of wisdom and virtue.

Only quite recently, however, historians have unearthed a working-class tradition that did not fit the regime's rhetorical codings—that of the Neapolitan cinema of the late 1910s and early 1920s, regionally defined and confined. By far the largest Italian city since the mid-nineteenth century, Naples had in fact developed a unique cinematic tradition capable of rendering its own vernacular version of "masses." Composed of impulsive, passionate, and destitute people entrenched in low-class street melodramas, these Neapolitan narrations were heavily censored and repressed by the nationalized film industry as dishonorable for the nation's image. Regional, plebeian stories and settings reemerged, however, during the neorealist period. And once again, they met the censorial practices of the newly established Christian Democratic government, unwilling to tolerate an embarrassing display of the false promises and abuses of postwar politics and society.[3]

Silent Production and Dark City Melodrama: The Neapolitan Case
From its beginnings, Italian silent cinema was dependent mainly on the success it achieved in foreign markets. The greatest centers of production, Milan, Turin, and Rome, were extremely
quick to structure their output according to the international
demand both in terms of genre and style. Historical/mythologi-
cal films, comedies, and what Salvador Dali later termed "le cinéma hystérique"4 (embodied in convoluted plots crowded with
femmes fatales, ruined aristocrats, and immoral dandies) represented the bulk of Italian movies up to the early 1920s. As a
result, mainly for the excessively precocious success of the star
system and the internationally acknowledged national craft in
historical settings and mass scenes, historical epics and sensual
bourgeois *feuilletons* were often wrongly considered to represent
the best examples of a truly working-class Italian film production.

Yet, already after World War I, these narrative and visual rou-
tines started showing an obsolescence that only film producers
decided to utterly disregard.5 The financial failure of the first
Italian film trust, UCI (Unione Cinematografica Italiana) created in 1919 and already defunct by 1926,6 symbolized the dark-
est period of an industry incapable of rationalizing and recuper-
ating its investments and in a deep crisis of stylistic identity.
Meanwhile, the Italian audience was applauding French and,
mainly, American films—which increasingly dominated the
domestic market. Still, two highly stylized genres retained some
popularity among the Italian audience after the war: the so-
called "athletic-acrobatic" one (featuring "strong men" such as
Maciste, Saetta, Ercole, and Sansone)—which narrated and glo-
rified the strength and beauty of the male hero's body—and the
crime-story serials of *Za-la-Mort*, which featured Emilio Ghione
in the Italian version of *Les Vampires* (such as *Anime buie* [Dark
Souls, 1916], *Il triangolo giallo* [The Yellow Triangle, 1917], and *I
topi grigi* [The Grey Mice, 1918]).

Most Italian cinema of this period hardly left the studio. Very
few scenes (natural scenes, car chases, transitional shots) were
shot outdoors, and even fewer captured the suburban areas or
the outskirts of the main centers (mainly revolving around past
imperial glories or morbid attractions of urban life).7 The only
cinematic tradition that consistently attempted to devote its

poetics to a real-life rendering of "suburban" stories was the Neapolitan one, which was consistently reprimanded by northern critics for its "excessive moods." In Naples, "suburban" did not merely refer to a "setting" spatially and culturally distant from the mannerly and affected style of contemporary decadent productions or the later "white telephone" tradition. Rather it referred to a peculiar way to reproduce a specific regional humanity.

Since the first years of the century, Neapolitan production companies such as Partenope Film, Vesuvio Films, and Films Dora resorted to a cinema *en plein air* by adopting "open-studio" sets and including documentary footage (*immagini dal vero*), thus disclosing a picturesque and plebeian world of back streets, urchins, working-class festivities and underclass *masques* typical of Neapolitan working-class culture.[8] The excessive and irreverent realism of such "ethnic" cityscapes, crammed with nonprofessional actors and thick symbolism and displaying morbid ventures of passion, death, and revenge, was unacceptable to the nationalistic and Apollonian demands of the Fascist cultural project. The city's unglamorous poverty and overt neglect for its children could not be part of the new "visual system," proudly termed "*nazional-popolare.*"

In the following years, technology wound up censoring the Neapolitan productions more effectively than the state bureaucracy. The introduction of sound in the film industry took Naples and its suburban slums away from the national scene. Sound equipment came to Naples only in the mid-1930s, and by that time, the creation of a central administrative body, the Direzione Generale de Cinematografia, and the competition of the government-controlled and technologically updated studios of Cinecittà had already tamed Naples's unacceptable cultural difference.

Antisuburban Cinema:
No-Man's-Land Between *Strapaese* and *Stracittà*

In several cultural and educational realms, Italy's Fascist regime attempted to address and "nationalize" the population according to the most "natural" criteria: age and gender. But the regime's newly nationalized working-class culture showed limits of ambiguity and contradiction. Its intrinsic polarizations, praising both the radical values of modernity, technology, and progress on the one hand, and the conservative attitude toward Italy's glorious antiquity and rural tradition on the other, originated an indeterminate disposition toward the present. As an aesthetic and poetic mood intrinsically tied to current concerns, authentic realism was not attainable for Fascist cinema, caught between a majestic past and a radiant future to be conquered.

Ideologically, in fact, Italian movies produced between 1922 and 1943 catalyzed a chasm of cultural and class representations. Upper bourgeois life-styles, oftentimes transposed in decadent and ludicrous fashions, were contrasted to rural settings, where virtue and innocence were "naturally" located. Not many narratives and stylistic endeavors were devoted to the increasingly widespread conditions of suburban humanities. As a result, by juxtaposing modernity and tradition, cinema's cultural operations appeared even more akin to the regime's ambiguous constituency and its politics of class segregation. This is especially true in light of Fascist innovative housing policies: the regime engaged in physically renovating and gentrifying cities' historical downtown districts[9] while developing suburban circles for the low-income tenants who could then live closer to healthfully isolated, pastoral locations.[10]

The need to associate the political ascent of Fascism with the rhetorical rescue of a newly fabricated rural "tradition" was only one dimension of Italy's cultural modernism—other tensions, proudly and aggressively self-stamped "modernist," were also part of the game. Caught between its Left or "revolutionary" nature and its conservative or "normalizing" elements, Fascism regarded ruralism and the preservation of the national tradition as the exemplary countermove against modern and dehumanizing life-styles. Yet, and by the same token, the regime's revolutionary ideals were a true challenge and a step forward from the shameful liberal and "anti-virile" past that humiliated Italy after the end of World War I.

In this cultural atmosphere, such opposition was summed up by two expressions: *strapaese* (ultra-country) and *stracittà* (ultra-city), which defined divergent but coexisting literary directions of the Fascist era.[11] *Strapaese* defended the national and traditional culture against the invasion of foreign, modern life-styles, and it became aligned with the regime's political ideals

AMBIGUOUS SOVEREIGNTIES

(and necessities) of commercial autarchy, cultural authenticity, and nationalistic pride.[12] *Stracittà* combined literary nationalism with prewar futurist enthusiasm for the machine age. Interestingly, these elitist avant-garde movements found themselves in line with the regime's need for a massive revival of the Italian culture on the international scene.

What is crucial in both the ideological fabrics of *strapaese* and *stracittà* and in the cinematic output they differently (and ambiguously) influenced is the disjunction of the Italian landscape into two poles: country/city, rural milieu/urban space, provincial and low-brow culture/international and sophisticated jet set, *borgo rurale/Grand Hotel*. Within such ideological antagonism, the poetics and geographies of reality in most films appear extremely unstable. Either they manifest a nostalgic attitude for a mythologized, distant past (ancient Rome, *Risorgimento* insurrections, or the regime's beginning, but also Italy's palingenetic rural and chaste tradition) or a longing for a brilliant future (modernization, an unknown interclass harmony and material well-being, or new cities and leisure activities) that appears on the horizon but is still largely unrealized.

This ideological instability was often registered by the cinema through a "spatial transit," a move from the city to the (paternal/maternal) countryside—with no significant stops in between. Such movement of returning to an old or finding a new home was quite commonly used as a narrative trajectory to show a journey of regeneration in films such as Mario Camerini's *Rotaie* (Rails, 1929), Alessandro Blasetti's *Terra Madre* (Mother Earth, 1931), and Amleto Palermi's *La peccatrice* (The Sinful Woman, 1940). In other cases, instead of a permanent move, the transition was a temporary one, and yet still capable of affecting the characters' lives. One-day excursions, a short holiday, or a business trip were the main narrative impetuses in films such as Raffaello Matarazzo's *Treno Popolare* (Popular Train, 1933), Mario Mattoli's *La dama bianca* (The Woman in White, 1938), and A. Blasetti's *Quattro Passi fra le Nuvole* (A Walk Among the Clouds, 1942). In other instances, the city was briefly left behind in order to better court a young woman as in Camerini's *Gli Uomini che Mascalzoni* (Men, What Rascals, 1932), or to forget the hopeless love for a decadent and promiscuous femme fatale, as in Augusto Genina's *Lo Squadrone Bianco* (The White Squadron, 1936).

At least in two instances—the only ones we know about among fictional films—the tension of modernization was effectively narrativized.[13] The construction of a new city or settlement embodied a gesture of progress and civilization. In 1929, Alessandro Blasetti's debut, *Sole* (Sun), filmed the paternalistic endeavor of Fascist agricultural and urban planning to refurbish and discipline antiquated and miserable living habits in sites of promiscuity, vice, and debauchery.[14] *Sole* was the first film to be considered part of the "Italian cinema renaissance"—a common motto among film critics after the financial and industrial crisis of the early 1920s. A later example was Domenico Paolella's *Gli ultimi della strada* (The Last Ones in the Street, 1940), interestingly set in a degraded Neapolitan milieu.[15]

Many other films of the period do not juxtapose narratively (and ethically) the city with the countryside. Instead, they are set in urban environments, like Camerini's *I Grandi Magazzini* (Department Stores, 1937), or *Il Signor Max* (Mr. Max, 1937), where the main character always plays with urbane manners or aristocratic moods. In these examples, what consistently emerges is an important trope of the Fascist suburban discourse: the impossibility of class mobility and interclass encounters. Any attempt to change roles or to enter spaces beyond one's own territory is bound to fail, and must be, at any rate, kept secret. True love and companionship exist only among class peers and within one's environment.

Later films produced in the early 1940s and set in premodern *borghi rurali* insist on the same point. Mario Soldati's *Piccolo Mondo Antico* (Small Antique World, 1941) and *Malombra* (1942) and Vittorio De Sica's *Un Garibaldino al Convento* (A Red Shirt at the Convent, 1942) depict the class rigidity of nineteenth-century Italian society as a Gothic and repressive setting. In *Piccolo Mondo Antico*, for instance, which takes place among aristocrats and high bourgeois members during the 1848 insurrections, the rise of Italy's nationalistic cause catalyzed an unprecedented sense of community and solidarity.

Yet, and once more, what several of these films did not (or could not) point to was a true and lasting possibility of class cohesion. The Fascist corporate state was a forced alliance of different classes and social needs, not their blending together. Every citizen and every social exchange had to preserve well-established social ranks; the Fascist city as the Fascist society was rigidly zoned and coded. Not by chance, in fact, the populist realism of these films was rather harmless and reactionary; it rested on frequent satire for aristocratic, decadent, and extravagant habits and bourgeois ephemeral intellectualism, all quite pernicious to virile action and contrary to "common sense." The ideological focus of these films, while constantly aiming at the dull lives of lonely patricians, failed to address the true dramas of the underprivileged ones.

In particular, a *critical* representation of the social difficulties and class conflicts of the present time—something that neorealism later developed at length—was utterly missing. The economic depression of the early 1930s, confronted by the regime with a reduction of jobs and wages, posed a direct threat to the national interclass cohesion. And yet, these social tensions were not registered by the cinema, whose romantic realism continued to be more wishful than accurate.

Hunger, Job Hunting, and a Cinema of the Present: The Poetic Hazards of Neorealism

In 1952 forty percent of the Italian labor force derived their income from agriculture, while only thirty percent drew theirs from industry. Ten years later, the percentages were reversed: thirty-nine percent of Italian workers were employed in industry, only twenty-seven in agriculture. Italy's industrialization was unbalanced; most of the industries were concentrated in the north while the south remained largely undeveloped. One million workers moved from the south to Rome or to the industrial centers of the north. From 1958 to 1961 Rome received more than 200,000 migrants, growing from 1,961,000 to 2,181,000. Milan had 1,274,000 inhabitants in 1951; in 1967 it had 1,681,000. Turin, the site of the booming Fiat factories, ballooned from 719,000 to 1,124,000.[16] The Italian economic boom invested the urban areas, often deepening the problems that Fascist housing policies had left unresolved. The middle class began to move out of the decaying historical downtowns to high rises located in protected communities outside the city center. The Fascist *borgate* received the bulk of the migrants from the countryside. They expanded, and progressively absorbed former *borghi rurali* (rural towns) into the boundaries of the newly enlarged cities.

Neorealist cinema devoted fresh critical attention to the "peripheral subjects" inhabiting these hinterlands. Often resorting to narrative metaphors of inclusion/exclusion, neorealism unearthed the deep social disjunctions of postwar Italian society. This novel sensitivity was not limited to Luchino Visconti's or Roberto Rossellini's groundbreaking early works, but was part of a shared aesthetic consciousness that pervaded intellectual and professional communities inside the Italian "film factory."

Many neorealist directors had been film critics and theorists. Trained as contributors to prestigious film periodicals such as *Bianco e Nero* and *Cinema*, they formulated new encounters between art and life far beyond the previous formulation of decadentism, or futurism. And they did so in the name of a new expressive realism, which inspired them to aim their cameras at those streets, city quarters, and "social subjects" that the "cinema under Fascism" had never been allowed to represent. Suburban unemployment and hunger, frequent abuse of children and elderly people, and the lack of legitimate opportunities made their way into the national representation of the newly liberated (and thus "open") cities.

Cinema finally registered the miserable lives of marginal characters living at the outskirts of Italian modernity, with no native, rural home—that is, no moral resource—to which to return. The opposition *strapaese/stracittà* had juxtaposed different values, and, in fact, had reproduced the omissions and the social and economic contradictions of the Fascist corporate society. The neorealist city, on the contrary, showed the human dramas of an economic civil war that pervaded every section of the city, sparing no "safety zones" but mostly affecting the weakest social figures (children and the elderly). For a brief but significant time, the typical scenery of neorealist cinema was a widely spread postwar city, a terrain of deep social contradictions and class conflicts, of human struggle and bleakness.

For the first time, films displayed situations and stories that explicitly attempted to build up a sense of national and working-class identity without deleting—as Fascist cinema had done—linguistic and historical specificities. Rossellini's *Paisà* (Paisan, 1946), for instance, devoted each episode (including the seventh, never completed) to a specific Italian region. Rossellini used the different dialects spoken by the film's characters to increase the sense of truth of the ambiance. While the film's unifying narrative frame stressed the commonalty of a troubled present, its unreconciled multilingualism emphasized Italy's geographical and historical diversity.[17]

Postwar Italian cinema showed peripheral and displeasing biographies instead of lingering on modern or archeological attractions of the downtown areas. Among these disturbing stories are those of wretched individuals, as in Rossellini's *Roma Città Aperta* (Open City, 1946); frail and powerless fathers, as in De Sica's *Ladri di Biciclette* (Bicycle Thieves, 1948); or lonely and destitute retirees, as in *Umberto D* (1952), again by De Sica. The favorite and most dramatic protagonists of the period are abandoned or neglected kids, as in Giuseppe De Santis's *I bambini ci guardano* (The Children Are Watching Us, 1943), De Sica's *Sciuscià* (Shoeshine, 1946), and even Visconti's *Bellissima* (Beautiful, 1951).

The "cinema during Fascism" had told stories of existential regeneration through the characters' transition from the city to the countryside. Neorealism, instead, polemically revealed the dramatic inequality between the downtown areas and the "humanistic," suburban outposts. If the commerce, bourgeois indifference, and modern decor of the city center sounded loud and hostile to the destitute neorealist characters, their misery and daily struggles amid the lousy apartment buildings of the periphery threatened to destroy their individual dignity. The sense of radical estrangement from the central urban circle was narratively exemplified by the neorealist characters' endless, daily walks or bus rides. In films like *Sciuscià* and *Ladri di Biciclette*, for instance, the main protagonists spend hours moving from their homes to the downtown areas.

In visualizing the increasing barriers between the different areas of the city, neorealism consciously reflected the social discrepancies of the Italian economic boom. The 1950s were a period of large profits, but also of extensive social losses, the former mostly privatized, the latter increasingly socialized. Unwilling to devolve any substantial part of the new income produced by the booming factories to the solution of urban problems, Italian governments postponed the formulation of a national housing plan until 1971. Between 1948 and 1963, only sixteen percent of what was spent in the construction industry went to building working-class housing. Italian cities, unequipped to accommodate the new dwellers, left them outside, in the *case popolari* (working-class housing projects) developed throughout the cities, or in the bidonvilles occupying the margins of the new cities. In 1952, a nonpartisan parliamentary inquiry discovered that 93,054 Romans lived in shacks, caves, or cellars.[18] Northern cities like Milan developed their own version of the *borgate*: the *coree* of the Milanese outskirts.

Italian cinema forcefully reacted to and reflected the changes that were radically transforming the physiology and topography of Italian cities. In a direct and polemical stance against the silence of Fascist cinema, the program of neorealism represented marginalized people and their stories. The problem was, however, how to represent them. They were indeed a new phenomenon. No longer peasants and not yet blue collars, the postwar *borgatari* hardly fit the categories of Italian, rigid Marxism, which were predominant among the major exponents of Italian cinema. Who were they? Were they the future? Or did they represent the past?

The new areas of the cities were often explored and theorized according to older binomies such as city/countryside or, better yet, factory workers/peasants. For Carlo Lizzani, a director close to the Italian Communist Party, neorealism reflected a society still "characterized by rural issues and their articulations." In reference to De Sica's *Sciuscià*, Lizzani noted that the city "around the characters is solely hell. Vision of redemption: the white horse, that is, an image evoking nature, countryside, liberty." To step out further than neorealism meant for some filmmakers to embrace with more heart the course of modernity, and to give more space to the factory workers. Lizzani's first feature, *Achtung, Banditi* (Achtung, Bandits, 1951) was the story of

AMBIGUOUS SOVEREIGNTIES

Genoese blue-collar workers and partisans fighting against Nazis to preserve the Italian factories, thus Italy's modern future. It was "the only Italian film [of the period] where the new balance of power is foreseen as destined to make the history of our country in the following twenty years—a balance that has an essential polarity in the presence of the working class."[19]

In pursuing the disturbing Italian "present" of the *borgate*, which Fascism had so successfully obscured, the neorealists found themselves in the awkward position of wishing away its "presence." True to their notion of cinema as an instrument of reform, many of them envisioned the act of "representing" the *borgate* as a necessary step leading to their elimination. The world of the *borgate* was—hopefully—a temporary situation, something in between the Fascist past and a better future, which their cinema was contributing to bring about. As a result, the spatial "movement" of so many characters of these films expressed not merely the reality of geography, but the ideal itinerary of history. "It would be a problem," argued De Santis in 1955, "if the forward-looking march (*cammino in avanti*) of the defeated factory worker in *Ladri di Biciclette*—and that of the artist—was not the same as the one of so many other workers who in the reality of the history of Italy were walking the same roads, not defeated by pessimism or fatalism, but engaged in the struggle to conquer a job."[20]

Based on the transformative power of cinema, neorealist eschatology envisioned the *borgate* as transitory, and it was hardly equipped to deal with their permanence. Their permanence marked neorealism's failure to promote change via their denunciation of the Italian troubled "present." In one revealing case, the *borgate* were literally made to disappear by magic in De Sica's *Miracolo a Milano* (Miracle in Milan, 1950). Realizing the impossibility of finding a solution to their problems within the city and yet unwilling to remain where they were, De Sica's marginalized Milanese abandon their bidonville by flying away on magical brooms. Such solutions were not limited to cinema. Unable to solve the housing crisis and eliminate the "shame" of the *borgate*, Italian governments resorted to some magic too. According to government statistics, in fact, the existence of the *borgate* was rarely recorded, a veritable nonevent. A 1970 report discovered 400,000 Romans living in houses that, according to official records, did not exist.[21]

And yet, *borgate* and *coree* were there and did not go away. Italian cities were no longer the ordered entities that they might have been, nor was their future reorganization easily attained. The social apartheid enforced by Fascism continued *de facto* in postwar Italian cities. In this context, then, the legacy of neorealism meant that the most sensitive Italian directors took into account the permanence of the "present," its stubborn "presence." The *borgate*—and their *Doppelgänger*, the middle-class high rises outside of the city centers—were not as transitory as neorealists had hoped. They actually sedimented. In the eyes of directors like Pier Paolo Pasolini and Michelangelo Antonioni, they originated a permanent and autonomous set of values and cultural issues. Time had come for a cinema that built on their "presence" rather than away from it.

Where the City (and the Cinema) Begins Again: Pasolini, Antonioni, and the Collapse of Neorealism

While the booming *borgate* changed the Italian cityscape, Italian culture was itself on the verge of change. "I am here to bury Italian Realism,"[22] declared Pasolini at the Open Gate Club in Rome during a debate about the Strega Literary Prize in 1960. If literature was detaching itself from the realistic *lingua franca*, some of the Italian directors were rethinking the neorealist paradigm, often far in advance of Italian film critics.

In this context, new solutions were to be expected. In fact 1960 and 1961 were the *anni mirabiles* of Italian cinema, and also of the cinematic representation of the new city. Federico Fellini's *La Dolce Vita* (The Good Life, 1960), Visconti's *Rocco e i suoi fratelli* (Rocco and His Brothers, 1960), and Pasolini's *Accattone* (Beggar, 1961) all embodied attempts to tell the story of these new Italian cities. *Rocco e i suoi fratelli*, a grim melodrama about a family from Calabria moving to the outskirts of Milan and featuring international stars such as Katina Paxinou of *For Whom the Bell Tolls* and Alain Delon, was awarded a prize at the 1960 Venice Film Festival. Fellini's *La Dolce Vita* won the Palm d'Or at the Cannes Film Festival. Compared with these two films, by two stars of Italian cinema, Pasolini's *Accattone* came last and—apparently—least. And yet, with *Accattone*, Pasolini radically reshaped the Italian cinematic representation of the proletarian *borgata*, representing it not merely as a site of oppression to be transformed and eliminated, but as the context where new, oppositional values were forged. After this movie, neorealism was indeed buried.

Pasolini was not a famous director then. He had written screenplays (among others, for Mario Soldati, Mauro Bolognini, and Federico Fellini), poems (both in Italian and in the Friulan dialect), and two controversial novels, *Ragazzi di vita* (Children of Life, 1955) and *Una vita violenta* (A Violent Life, 1959). Both novels dealt with the same milieu as *Accattone*, the Roman *borgate*, the large spaces opening up at the margins of the metropolis "where one thinks the city ends and where instead it begins again"—as Pasolini wrote in one of his poems, "Sesso: consolazione della miseria" (Sex: Consolation for Misery).[23] *Accattone* did not do well at the Venice Film Festival where it premiered 30 August 1961. Censors threatened cuts, and critics—even progressive ones—did not fully endorse the film, or at least not as much as they had endorsed *Rocco*.[24]

As opposed to the transitional *borgata* of neorealist cinema and Visconti's *Rocco e i suoi fratelli*, Pasolini suggested that the *limen* of the city was a character equipped with its own determination to be present, to speak.[25] In *Accattone*, Vittorio, nicknamed "Accattone," is a pimp living in a Roman *borgata* (the film was shot mostly in the *borgate* of Torpignattara and Pigneto). The film follows his fate as he loses his woman, Maddalena, to the jail, falls in love with another, Stella, tries to work for a day, quits his job, and eventually dies while trying to steal some hams. It was—more or less—the same story as *Ragazzi di vita*, Pasolini's controversial novel about the young *borgataro* Riccetto. Yet, cinema now afforded Pasolini a new possibility. As a language of "presence," Pasolini told Adriano Aprá, cinema is not representation of life but "the written manifestation of reality."[26]

Pasolini's cinema "roots" the bodies of his characters in their landscape. Those *gagliardi* (vigorous) bodies celebrated in the novels came to life in the film.[27] Emphasizing the *productive* rather than the *representational* power of cinema, Pasolini unleashed what neorealismo and Visconti had kept under control through the mechanism of the melodrama. In *Rocco*, Visconti's cinema functioned as the progressive avenger, lambasting Milan for oppressing the brothers who are first and foremost victims of their brutal surroundings. Victimization and melodrama, on the contrary, are resisted by Accattone and his cohort.[28] In the end, when Accattone is about to die on the street curb, the anti-hero refuses to concede defeat or to die according to melodramatic conventions. Instead, he again reclaims his active role in the making of his fate. *"Mo' sto bene"* (Now, I am fine), he sneers.

Even from the screen the *borgatari* managed to be disruptive. Pasolini seems continuously on the verge of losing control, not only of the camera—the "wrong editing" and the "felt camera" that characterizes the cinema of poetry—but of the actors themselves. Chasing realism, Visconti chose professional actors for *Rocco*,[29] but Pasolini's *Accattone* was peopled by non-professionals, his friends from the *borgate*, the Citti brothers, Mario Cipriani, Polidor (whom he pitted together with his other friends), and the bourgeois intellectuals Adele Cambria and Elsa Morante. During the shooting, Franco Citti (who played the lead) was arrested by the police for a petty crime and many actors threatened to leave the set, perhaps annoyed with the only professional on the set, cinematographer Tonino delli Colli.[30]

Unleashed by Pasolini, Vittorio and his friends refuse to consider their *borgata* as a simple transition devoid of culture, values, and resistance. It was not that Pasolini failed to understand the injustice underlying the reality of the *borgata*. But the director was uncertain whether the world outside of the *borgata*, engrossed in its own dreams of consumerism, discipline and police violence had really something to teach the *borgatari*. It was the violent "Italietta" of the summer of 1960, that of the uncurbed violence of the "Scelba squads," and of the right-wing Tambroni government, which the film implicitly evoked as a sort of hidden context, especially in the scene when Vittorio is arrested by a brutal police squad. The *borgata* becomes an urbanistic "in-between," generating its own set of values and priorities, its own language (a version of the Roman dialect), its own resistances to the dominant ideology of work, state, police, and church. In *Accattone*, the hero's ultimate inability to work in a scrap metal depot becomes a rejection of the alienating dimension of work in a capitalist, labor-intensive society. "Oh!?," he cries out, "Is this Buchenwald?" Similarly Pasolini's *Uccellacci Uccellini* (Hawks and Sparrows, 1966) does not celebrate the heroes of the bourgeois culture but those of the *borgata*, as expressed in the fictional street signs: "Via Lillo Strappalenzuola—who escaped from home when he was 12," "Via Benito La Lacrima—unemployed," "Via Antonio Mangiapasta—garbage man."

Pasolini's cinema remained grounded in the *borgata* throughout the filmmaker's early career. *Mamma Roma* (1962), with Anna Magnani in the title role of the former prostitute who reforms to offer her son a better future, was set in the Roman outskirts of Ceccafumo. After *Mamma Roma*, Pasolini's cinema cited the *borgata* as the place of the "sacred." He used one of the oldest Italian *borgate*, the caves of Matera, as the stand-in of Jesus' Palestine in *Il Vangelo secondo Matteo* (The Gospel according to St. Matthew, 1964), the Appia Antica as a background of a contemporary Passion in "La Ricotta" (an episode of *Rogopag*, 1963), and the no-man's-land surrounding Rome's airport of Fiumicino as the setting for the political/religious meditations of *Uccellacci Uccellini*.

If the cinema of Pasolini dwelled on the anthropological extinction of nonintegrated, unresolved, and "not reconciled" human figures, surviving at the spatial and cultural outskirts of the modern city, Michelangelo Antonioni, instead, ventured in the bourgeois residential suburbs, where the unreconciled subject is a mute elegant woman (such as Monica Vitti) whose charge of silence and crisis unbearably disturbs the obtuse psychological balance of her busy partner.[31] Like Accattone, however, Antonioni's characters are a result of modern processes of industrialization. They are not outsiders, as Pasolini's subproletarians, but insiders, fully created and deeply affected by the cultural reorientations brought about by modern lifestyles. Antonioni's female characters, in fact, display an emotive uneasiness and anxiety as unknown to neorealist narrations as their elegant, modernly furnished, suburban apartments.

Although culturally and professionally formed among 1940s directors, screenwriters, and critics, Antonioni cannot be considered simply a proponent of some sort of neorealist psychologism—a later, inward extension of the more traditional neorealist sociologism—as he was perceived at the beginning of his career. His attitude toward the classic neorealist poetics was as dissident and problematic as Pasolini's. Both authors, in fact, often showed deep personal concerns for film style and an interest for characters and subjects—upper bourgeois in Antonioni and proletarian in Pasolini—programmatically excluded or stereotyped by neorealist narrations.[32]

By gazing inside the luxurious and yet morally uncomfortable spaces of the new Italian upper bourgeoisie, Antonioni not only introduced new subjects, or devoted entire narrations to them, but he also radically modified the way in which a film story could be told. His preference for existential anti-dramatization and his lingering shots on silent characters and empty spaces utterly conflated with the neorealist sound identification of social dialectics and dramaturgy.[33] One of the most effective ways in which the director of L'Avventura (The Adventure, 1959) achieved his representation of the "malady of the present" is through a peculiar rendering of spaces, urban landscapes, and suburban *terrain vagues*.

In his first films one still observes traditional neorealist tropes, such as the critique of social and class conflicts in terms of failed integrations, especially in Cronaca di un amore (Chronicle of a Love, 1950) and I vinti (The Vanquished, 1952), but also in La signora senza camelie (Lady Without Camellias, 1953) and Le amiche (Girlfriends, 1955). In the productions of the late 1950s and early 1960s, instead, Antonioni explored the precarious lives of his characters amid the new spaces of the factory, its undefined and desolate surroundings, and its deserted peripheral motor intersections or suburban crossroads, which he converted into the "objective correlatives" of modern anxiety.

Often, the "primary scene" of his cinema is a woman living through an emotional crisis, who, lonely and confused, walks across an empty street. Her solitude could be "diegetic" and episodic, as Lidia's in La notte (The Night, 1961), who wanders about Sesto San Giovanni, Milan's furthest periphery, but also Vittoria's in L'eclisse (Eclipse, 1962), or Giuliana's in Deserto rosso (Red Desert, 1964), who are filmed while walking aimless-

AMBIGUOUS SOVEREIGNTIES

ly around their peripheral domiciles. The main character's lone-liness may also be a perennial state of utter isolation and remoteness, even in the presence of her partner, as for Claudia in *L'Avventura*.

In Antonioni's poetic system, it matters where characters meet or fail to meet. While Fascist or neorealist characters met in downtown crowded squares or main streets, in *L'eclisse* the two lovers have an appointment in an anonymous street corner at EUR, the fancy new suburban quarter built in Rome and designed by Fascist architects a few decades before. The very location of their encounter, a motor intersection, is more than a set; it is the predicament of a broader existential metaphor. Stylistically, Antonioni is thus able to upgrade the spatial con-figuration of the city and its districts (sometimes including its noises—always its silence) to a fundamental narrative figure and eloquent visual component. The mere architectural lines of the residential suburban crossroads and buildings become char-acters of their own. Their alienating and peripheral constituen-cy becomes, in the long run, a sinister reminder of an over-whelming despair and isolation.

Epilogue: Progressive Cinema as Tourism

In the last twenty years, Italy's society, like most other Western ones, has witnessed a progressive gentrification of its formerly diverse class structure. Italian cinema has mainly depicted bour-geois atmospheres and stories—whose dramatic intimacy and agoraphobic, oppressive settings were pioneered by Antonioni's stylized cinema. Rarely has the national film culture followed Pasolini's example. The *borgate* remain part of Italian cinema, but few filmmakers have perceived them as an autonomous universe, generating their own set of alternative values.

The questions posited by Pasolini's cinema often were beyond the reach, or the interests, even of those progressive filmmakers who sided—like Pasolini—with the Italian Left. Ettore Scola's *Brutti Sporchi e cattivi* (Ugly, Dirty, and Evil, [released in English as *Down and Dirty*], 1976), revisited the places of Pasolini's cinema to tell the story of *borgataro* Giacinto Mazzatella. Given a million lire by an insurance company after losing an eye in an accident, Giacinto is besieged by his greedy relatives who want to eliminate him and get their hands on the insurance money. After surviving a nearly successful attempt at his life, Giacinto shoots one of the relatives, sets fire to the family's shack, and sells the family land to a group of Calabrians. Ultimately, Giacinto has his money glued to his body in a cast while the Calabrians and his family are forced to share the same home. Set in one of the Roman *borgate* next to Saint Peter's Cathedral, the film employed one of Pasolini's historical collaborators, Sergio Citti, as dialogue consultant. Pasolini himself was supposed to appear in a filmed preface to the movie, commenting on the barbarism that had invested all aspects of society. He was, however, unable to do this. In November 1975, the filmmaker/poet/novelist was killed by one of his "ragazzi di vita," Pino Pelosi, at the Idroscalo Ostiense of Rome, one of those *borgate* whose "sacred presence" he celebrated. What he saw of Scola's film and its script, however, did not convince him. *Brutti Sporchi e cattivi*, again, saw the *borgatari* as the victims of an increasingly barbaric and materialistic society. For the film, Pasolini wished a bleaker ending, insofar as "the dwellers of the *borgate* are themselves responsible for their fate, because they have chosen to let themselves open to colonization and barbarization."[34]

Perhaps the unresolved contrast between the legacy of neorealism's civic, transformative cinema and Pasolini's complex relation to the *borgate* is contained in Nanni Moretti's *Caro Diario* (Dear Diary, 1993), both a homage to the cinema of Pasolini and Moretti's confession of his own different choices. Moretti's style—with its rejection of the melodrama and its penchant for nonprofessional actors, Roman settings, and conscious imperfections—reveals the director's debt to Pasolini. In the first episode of *Caro Diario*, "*In Vespa*," Moretti concludes his roaming about Rome in front of the place where Pasolini was murdered. Yet, while paying homage to him, *Caro Diario* also reveals that Pasolini's legacy is no longer a viable mode for Moretti's cinema. Like the neorealists, Moretti dreams of a cinema passionately engaged in contemporary political debates and capable of affecting the present. Visiting one of the latest of Roman *borgate*, Spinaceto, Moretti pokes fun at those who deny the deeply entrenched humanity of the place, and righteously

AMBIGUOUS SOVEREIGNTIES

"bad mouth" it, writing melodramatic scripts such as "Escape from Spinaceto." The place is "not bad," Moretti says. Yet, he cannot stay. Ill at ease in the presence of the suburban squalor, the director leaves almost immediately after arriving.

What Pasolini constructed as a "cinema of presence," Moretti ironically transforms into "a cinema of travel," a "touch-and-go" in which the progressive filmmaker remains openly external, an accidental tourist, though a progressive-minded one. Conscious of Pasolini's lesson, Moretti views the *borgata* as more than mere urban nightmare. But the director feels out of place. The *borgata* is "not bad," but Moretti still shares the reformist ideals and dreams of an engaged cinema. Spinaceto is a sign of oppression that—like the protected, peripheral, middle-class neighborhoods of Casalpalocco, which he also visits—denies and endangers the beauty of Rome. Spinaceto is, therefore, left behind in a hurry by the director whose camera is no longer able, or willing, to narrate it. Perhaps what he wants is still the *bellissima* Rome of the 1950s, which existed before the middle class abandoned its center, and the sub-proletarians were permanently confined into the *borgate*. But that "present"—if it ever was—is long gone. The unreformed "presence" of the *borgate* reminds him too much of the failure of Italian society to achieve those social changes that the neorealists thought of as attainable five decades ago. Better to get back on the Vespa and keep riding.

Moretti represents the remains of Pasolini, or at least his memory, via his final stop in front of the place where the poet/director died. But even there, his "presence" is eroded, more and more uncertain, and contested. The monument erected to his death is rapidly deteriorating.

1. For an extensive and informative discussion, see U.S. Work Progress Administration for the City of New York, Division of Foreign Housing Studies, *Data Concerning Housing Agencies in Italy: Their Functions and Organization*, second edition (New York: New York Housing Authority, 1938).

2. Among the several possible sources, see Bruno Moretti, *Case d'abitazione in Italia: Quartieri popolari, case operaie, case per impiegati* (Houses for Habitation in Italy: Working-Class Neighborhoods, Workers Houses, Employee Houses) (Milan: Hoepli, 1929).

3. On the role of Giulio Andreotti in the anti-neorealist polemic, see "Intervista all'ex sottosegretario Giulio Andreotti" (Interview with the Ex-Undersecretary Giulio Andreotti), in Alberto Farassino, *Neorealismo: Cinema italiano, 1945–49* (Neorealism: Italian Cinema, 1945–49) (Turin: EDT, 1989), 75–78.

4. Salvador Dali, *Abregé d'une Histoire critique du cinéma* (Summary of a Critical History of Cinema) (Paris: Ed. des Cahiers libres, 1932), later translated and quoted in Pietro Bianchi, *Francesca Bertini e le dive del cinema muto* (Francesca Bertini and the Divas of Silent Cinema) (Turin: Utet, 1969), 140.

5. For an overview of the industrial and narrative crisis that occurred after World War I, see Gian Piero Brunetta, *Storia del cinema italiano. Il cinema muto, 1895–1929* (History of Italian Cinema: Silent Cinema, 1895–1929) (Rome: Editori Riuniti), 231–37.

6. UCI was created in 1919 from an alliance of the majority of Italy's most prominent production companies. Financially supported by two leading banking institutions, the Italian Commercial Bank and the Italian Savings Bank, from the start UCI acted as a national monopoly capable of fighting back the American competition. During the 1919 and 1920 seasons, UCI produced as many as 150 films per year. In this effort, however, the Italian conglomerate showed irresponsible tendencies for developing gigantic plans of production without securing distribution and exhibition outlets and for squandering resources on excessively elaborate costume films and in exorbitant contracts to Italian film "stars." When their credit collapsed in 1922, UCI, and the entire Italian film industry, disintegrated.

7. An interesting exception is represented by a few of Ghione's films. For instance, *I topi grigi* shows, for purely narrative reasons, poor and isolated outposts (*borghi* and *borgate*) of early-twentieth-century Italian cities where underground mobs and gangs of thieves are accustomed to meet or forced to hide.

8. *Vedute* (views) was a common genre of Neapolitan cinema, especially suited for international export. For a general account, see Adriano Aprá, ed., *Napoletana: Images of a City* (Milan: Fabbri Editori, 1993). For a specific cultural investigation of one of the most important production companies, Films Dora, headed by Elvira and Nicola Notari, see Giuliana Bruno, *Streetwalking on a Ruined Map: Cultural Theory and the City Films of Elvira Notari* (Princeton, NJ: Princeton University Press, 1993).

9. A good example of this practice is represented by Milan. After 1922, the new Fascist city government, with the backing of the property owners' association, decided that downtown buildings were not to be rented anymore to working-class tenants, but were to be sold to middle-class ones or offered (for sale or for rent) to state bureaucrats and public employees at privileged rates. Extensive building programs were developed at the urban fringes to offer low-rent dwellings to those people "evicted" from the central core. See Thomas Angotti,

AMBIGUOUS SOVEREIGNTIES

Housing in Italy: Urban Development and Political Change (New York: Praeger Publishers, 1977), especially 35 ff., and 53–54.

10. At times, the urban planning system elaborated educational and paternalistic programs for families "of irregular composition, with poor moral background." Between 1924 and 1940, twenty-three outer neighborhoods, called *borgate*, were created in Rome. Each was located near a military installation in order to ensure state control over the civilian population. These *borgate* were not conceived as suburban settlements, as they later became in the postwar period, but as rural communities where families "in moral need" could "be reformed by honest country living (and the constant surveillance of the military)." The ideological, ethical, and patriarchal urge to recuperate "regionalism" and "agricultural values" over the sinister northern European industrialism and decadence had found a territorial translation. See Angotti, *Housing in Italy*, 34–35.

11. Initially "*stracittà*" was coined as a polemical buzzword, later proudly embraced and adopted by its adherents. For an overview of the cultural tensions and literary confrontations of the period, see Luciano Troisio, *Le riviste di Strapaese e Stracittà* (Journal of Ultra-Country and Ultra-City) (Treviso: Canova, 1975).

12. For a manifesto of the movement, see Mino Maccari, "Strapaese," *Il selvaggio* 4 (16 September 1927).

13. It must be reminded that, differently from fictional films, the pedagogical documentaries and propaganda newsreels produced by the state's Light Institute and mandatorily exhibited in every movie theater of the nation, extensively covered the Fascist "agricultural and urban revolution." Regularly, the inauguration of a new Fascist city built after widely publicized drainages was performed by the Duce himself. See for instance newsreels such as *Inaugurazione di Littoria* (18 December 1932), *Inaugurazione di Pomezia* (25 April 1938), or *Aprilia* (4 July 1938).

14. In *Sole*, a story of swamps being drained, the local opposition to the new agricultural and health reform is negatively represented as trivial, murderous, backward people who, in the end, are defeated by the enlightened and composed beauty of the chief engineer (master and "messiah" of industrial progress).

15. In this film, the Fascist "modern" pedagogical policies were, once more, embodied in the healthy and learned figure of the protagonist who, like that in *Sole*, rescues his female counterpart and marries her. Quite curiously, the film was an ideological remake of a Soviet film, *Putevka v zizn* (The Road to Life) directed in 1931 by Nikolaj Ekk. See Adriano Aprá, "Naples in Film (1930–1993): A Map," in Aprá, *Napoletana*, 98.

16. Paul Ginsborg, *History of Contemporary Italy* (London: Penguin, 1990), 218–20.

17. In contrast the Neapolitan film industry soothed and curbed its vernacular makeup by Italianizing the accent of its characters and keeping its working-class moods only for the characters' stereotypical gestures and their songs. Quite symptomatically, in 1947 two remakes of previous mid-1910s Neapolitan successes were made, *Assunta Spina* and *Sperduti nel buio* (Lost in the Darkness), as to emphasize the poetic continuity between silent Neapolitan cinema and the newly acclaimed neorealist mood. *Assunta Spina*, directed in 1915 by Gustavo Serena with Francesca Bertini, was remade by Mario Mattoli with Anna Magnani and Eduardo De Filippo; *Sperduti nel buio*, directed in 1914 by Nino Martoglio, was remade by Camillo Mastrocinque and featured Vittorio De Sica.

18. Ginsborg, *History of Modern Italy*, 187–88.

19. Carlo Lizzani, "Il Neorealismo: quando è finito quello che resta" (Neorealism: What Remains When it is Finished), in Lino Miccichè, ed., *Il Neorealismo Cinematografico Italiano* (Italian Cinematographic Neorealism) (Venice: Marsilio, 1975), 98–105. Our translation.

20. Giuseppe De Santis, "È in crisi il Neorealismo?" (Is Neorealism in Crisis?), *Filmcritica* 4 (March–April 1951), reprinted in Claudio Milanini, ed., *Neorealismo. Poetiche e polemiche* (Milan: Il Saggiatore, 1980), 136–43. Our translation.

21. Ginsborg, *History of Modern Italy*, 247.

22. Pier Paolo Pasolini, "In morte del realismo" (1960), reprinted in Milanini, *Neorealismo*, 236–41.

23. Pier Paolo Pasolini, "Sesso: consolazione della miseria" (Sex: Consolation for Misery), *Roman Poems*, trans. Lawrence Ferlinghetti and Francesca Valente (San Francisco: City Lights Books, 1986), 48.

24. See the adoring introduction to the film by the late Guido Aristarco—one of the deans of Italian film criticism—in Guido Aristarco and Gaetano Carancini, *Rocco e i suoi fratelli* (Bologna: Cappelli, 1960).

25. Paola Cabibbo has stressed the importance of liminal areas, what she calls the "in-between-ness," not as something merely auxiliary to the terms between which it is located, but as a bearer of its own values. In this sense, the "in-between-ness" represents the space "in which the dissolution of the traditional oppositions, before/after, reality/fiction, fiction/metafiction, is the founding element." Paola Cabibbo, "Spazi Liminali" (Liminal Space), in Paola Cabibbo, ed., *Lo Spazio e le sue rappresentazioni: Stati, modelli, paesaggi* (Space and Its Representation: States, Models, Landscape) (Naples: Edizioni Scientifiche Italiane, 1993), 13–38.

26. Pier Paolo Pasolini, "Quips on cinema," *Heretical Empiricism*, ed. Louise K. Barnett, trans. Ben Lawton and Louise K. Barnett (Bloomington: Indiana University Press, 1988), 225. See also Pier Paolo Pasolini, "La Fine dell'avanguardia," *Nuovi Argumenti* 3–4 (September 1962).

27. See Michele Mancini and Giuseppe Perella, *Pier Paolo Pasolini. Corpi e Luoghi* (Works and Places) (Rome: Theorema, 1981), 103.

28. On the relationship between Rocco's narrative structure and the melodrama see Pio Baldelli, *I Film di Luchino Visconti* (The Film of Luchino Visconti) (Milan: Mazzotta Editore, 1973), 202.

29. See Pier Paolo Pasolini, "Cinema of Poetry," in *Heretical Empiricism*, 167–86.

30. On the making of the film see Schwartz, *Pasolini Requiem*, 348–81.

31. For a brief overview of the city and its periphery in postwar Italian cinema, see Lino Miccichä, "La metafora della periferia nel cinema italiano del dopoguerra" (The Metaphor of the Periphery in Italian Postwar Cinema) in A. Clementi and F. Perego, eds., *Eupolis: La Riqualificazione delle città in Europa* (The Requalification of the City in Europe), vol. 1, "Periferia Oggi" (Rome-Bari: Laterza, 1990), 222–30.

32. Consider, for example, De Sica's *Miracolo a Milano* (Miracle in Milan, 1950).

33. It must be noted that Antonioni was one of the first Italian non-avant-garde directors to stylistically experiment with the narrative innovations performed by modern European literature after the turn of the century. Compare, for instance, Gustave Flaubert's obsession with style and form, James Joyce's sudden rupture or endless extension of the sentence/sequence or his attention for the continuum of memories and present accidents, Alain Robbe-Grillet's analytical gaze and

phenomenological investigation, Albert Camus's existential inquiry, F. Scott Fitzgerald's narrative settings, etc.

34. Pier Paolo Pasolini, cited in Roberto Ellerio, *Ettore Scola* (Florence: La Nuova Italia, 1988), 55. Our translation.

Giorgio Bertellini is a Ph.D. student in cinema studies at New York University. He has published essays in Film History, Film Quarterly, *and* NEMLA Italian Studies, *and is the author of* Emir Kusturica *(Milan: Editrice Il Castoro, 1996).*

Saverio Giovacchini is a Ph.D. student in history at New York University and has taught film studies and history at the University of Florence and New York Unversity. He has published essays on cinema, history, D. W. Griffith, and African-American cinema. His most recent essay, "Shoot the Right Thing: African-American Filmmakers and American Public Discourse," was included in Anna Maria Martellone, ed., Toward a New American Nation *(Boomon, England: Keele, 1995).*

Eyes That Do Not See

Yves Nacher and Françoise Zamour

Sometimes film fixes images, sometimes film is desperately empty. *Mon Oncle* (My Uncle, Jacques Tati, 1958) and *La Haine* (The Hate, Mathieu Kassovitz, 1995), two movies set forty years apart that reputedly portray the suburbs well, are studies of eyes that see and eyes that do not see.[1]

—Here, as you see, is the living room.

—But . . . it looks empty.

—Oh, it is modern; everything communicates.[2]

We are in the fifties, amid the myth of modern comfort, as seen in women's magazines, and the Salon des Arts Menagers.[3] Light and space at last! The living room is as big and warm as an airport lobby; its fake design and cute functionalist artifacts make the woman's mother-in-law and the neighbors turn pale with envy. Everyone, in particular the dear little bright faces, has a room. The bathroom is designed to trap the bacteria that could be obnoxiously hidden in a vicious pore. The kitchen is beyond even the craziest futurist's imagination; in it a Wagnerian symphony of appliances rival one another in noise and fury.

Mrs. Arpel, the guardian of this temple of certainty—seen constantly holding her rag, her finger compulsively gripping the trigger of an appliance, the acerbic heel of her perfect mother-and-wife pink mule slapping like a metronome the aseptic surface of a life too smooth—is, contrary to appearances, not Mrs.

Apartment interior, Saint-Denis

Everybody. Rather, she is the reflection of the dream of Mrs. Everybody, a modern center of healthy life, where the artifices of progress permanently support the loud carol of happiness.

No matter the pathological neurosis of the dachshund eternally wrapped in its checkered coat, the modern family must be forged one way or another, and the House of Tati is a mold that gives everyone a place in a new economic and social order. This is not a house anymore, it is the domestic manifestation of a panoptical utopia, a social and political rehabilitation camp ready to push into progress a society that, according to the people high up, was hungry for it.

Was Tati's eye so far from reality? Was modern vertigo created only for the fictions shown in dark rooms? Indeed, the trauma of World War II had created a deep desire for a *tabula rasa* in France in the fifties. France sought to forget that it was traditionally late in the race to modernity, and that it had been destroyed by the bombings. It tried to bury the taboos of a recent history hard to swallow, such as Vichy and collaboration. Nothing of the past must be kept. On a political and social level, as well as in the memory of forms, modern happiness had to be amnesiac. It also had to be original, and it had to be French, in order to recompose a social body destroyed by a collective enterprise of national awakening. Imbued with universalism, the prevailing ideas wanted to invent a shared modernity in the name of the common good and break away from a modern movement reputed to be reserved for the bourgeois elite. Thus the improvement of cities depended on an egalitarian program that favored unifying and standardizing design for the middle class. At a time when housing war victims and children of the baby boom and rural exodus was the priority, architecture focused on efficiency rather than style. Under the cover of health, cheap real estate, demographic pressure, and rationalization of building techniques, the building industry was inventing a new modernity that spawned lumplike rectangular concrete buildings, pathetic lawns, sad flower clumps, and endless suburbs of towers and slabs, thrown on the ground as in a huge and cynical construction game.

The same slabs can be seen at the end of the Arpel's street, right behind a row of "Arpelian" houses that look desperately fake. Most of the families that fled the suburban shantytowns or the city centers' run-down housing saw in the new suburbs their promised land, the key to legitimate happiness, or a revenge on their childhood, in which eight kids lived in six square feet of crowded quarters without running water while the parents spent their lives unfolding mattresses and cooking on portable gas stoves. As opposed to the new suburbanites, Tati made the choice of passive resistance. He chose Hulot over the hygienic banality of everyday life. Hulot was Mrs. Arpel's brother-in-law who did not fit in, who stubbornly refused to see or to understand, and whose unusual—and anti-Arpel—house was built in a prewar postcard-like French town, complete with red wine, accordions, an old motorbike, and the unavoidable umbrella. In short, Hulot was incapable of fitting his large body in the modern era as well as in the kidney-shaped armchairs of the Arpel house. Tati's questioning of modernity was not expressed in violence—this was not Tati's style—but rather as a recurring doubt, a kind of warning to anyone who wanted to hear it. Besides, there was little Gerard, the well-groomed mama's boy, the designated victim of modernity, carrying his cross in the cute non-city where his conscientious parents had sequestered him. (Forty years later, killed little by little by boredom, is he the bad boy in Kassovitz's *La Haine*?)

Through Hulot's eyes, Tati looked at the modern world like a spectator with a refined skepticism. Ten years later, events proved him right. In the early seventies, the collective dream of modernity became a nightmare. "Hell is the others," say the characters of the bittersweet comedies that came out on the French screens of the time. In them, urban dwellers—nostalgic for verdure—decide to realize the nineteenth-century absurd-loving writer Alphonse Allais's dream, to build cities in the country. Numerous movies, only a few of them worth remembering, illustrate the failure of this generous utopia as it was transformed into visits to the supermarket and neighbors snoring audibly through paper-thin walls. Cinema followed these consciences and adopted a new tone.

The first dysfunctions of the suburbs that had been born from a technocratic will appeared very quickly, and so a gaze that condemned modern architecture and those living in it was born. Critical at first, this gaze soon became mean, and embodied a failure that urban planners recognized without discussion.

Is the thunderous *La Haine* the answer to this latent meanness? Like *Mon Oncle*, it is a cult movie. But it transcended the genre to attract the youth from the suburbs (to whom an unavoidable advertising campaign promised immediate identification with the characters) as well as the bourgeois elite (ready for some sociological trills enhanced by Dolby sound). Is *La Haine* the *Mon Oncle* of a doubtful *fin de siècle*? This *fin de siècle* has good reasons for doubt. The ubiquitous housing projects (for, in its great generosity, the welfare state of the *Trente Glorieuses*[4] did not forget one square meter of the country, not even one embryonic middle-sized town) are collapsing, literally—after thirty years, the buildings are badly aging—and figuratively speaking. Unemployment, delinquency, drugs, criminality, police blunders—the problems, as well as the clichés, are numerous. This morose situation was given a name: the crisis of the suburbs.

Some people think that movies are a sociological reflection of reality. Among them is Kassovitz, who claims that in *La Haine* he shot an indictment of police brutality. His method is relentless. The movie opens in an anonymous suburban project with night shots of a car chase between the police and hooligans, alarmist TV news flashes, slow-motion explosions across the screen: the scene is set. Then the action accelerates, along with the rugged narrative, which is no more than a Pavlovian interpretation of twenty-four hours of an enclosed life, of a vicious circle doomed to remain perpetually rooted in the same spot. The film is shot in black-and-white to emphasize the claim that one is far from the picturesque or the bucolic (as if there was any doubt), although black-and-white is also the conventional aesthetic code of the nineties. The rhythm of the film is in between that of a music video and a commercial spot, which is the obligatory signature for a young prodigal movie maker immersed in his era. In the middle of all this are three puppets, one hothead, one coward, and one moralist—more specifically, one Jew, one black, one *beur*,[5] a scientifically determined sample of statistical unhappiness.

Is this chronicle of a flash revolt in a boiling suburban housing project—which takes place after a youngster is injured by

French housing under construction

the police and then hospitalized between life and death—really the portrait of a generation? More correctly, it is its antithesis. Where Tati used a prescient fiction and a pointillistic study of consciences, Kassovitz runs head down into a virtual reality truer than reality itself. He shoots the fate of destinies that hit the wall, an infernal circle of drifting lives, a recurring marginality that is inscribed in DNA.

This is the vulgarized contemporary thinking on suburban projects, a confusing mix of social vision trapped in its contradictions (how can we help them and at the same time help ourselves?) and its popular cultural imagery (the Nike sneakers and the other dress codes have been adopted quickly by the chic neighborhoods, for they go so well with the Hermès scarves). The tone varies between that of a naturalistic nihilistic documentary and CNN on acid. It is too much, and all these overdetermined signs of the so-called reality of the projects—the cops, all bad; the aesthetic of the graffiti; the score, a mix of reggae, hip hop, and project slang that wants to imitate the Bronx, but is too well written to be true—make us doubt its authenticity. Something prompts us to resist the view. The artificiality is so much stronger than the reality, or the so-called reality, that one finally gives up. The suburb is reduced to a simple narrative and visual "background noise"; it has become part of a game of connotations cut from their references.

Kassovitz claims that his movie is a documentary. It is that, indeed, but its subject is not the one he thinks it is. The reality he shot is not that of the suburbs, but of the well-to-do urban-dweller's gaze on unchecked growth. Very few people can call themselves authentic suburban kids, and Kassovitz is not one of them. His life is somewhere else, and so is his gaze. Kassovitz's eye reflects not the chronicle of an actor of urban fears and of guilty repressions, but that of a spectator. *La Haine* is not a movie about the suburban project. It is only a movie about how the project is represented by people who look at it only through screens, people who are terrorized by the idea that, because of an unfortunate circumstance, they could get lost while driving across such *terrae incognitae*.

Some people celebrated too quickly the cultural crowning of these cursed no-man's-lands. French cinema, with very few exceptions, is still unable to have a normal relationship with these territories. It still sees them marked by the original sin of the radical political and social thinking that spawned them, and that still wreak havoc. French cinema is unable to project in these territories ordinary destinies and stories, unable to free itself from the journalistic or aesthetic clichés of the moment, and unable to get rid of the feeling of extra-territoriality that will not dissipate as long as the social body itself does not learn how to face its problems, its guilt, and its repressions.

Graham Greene invented the "travels with my aunt"; did the travel with *Mon Oncle* lead to the wall? It is clear that, as Italo Calvino invented his invisible cities, France has invented invisible suburbs. They are invisible because nobody knows how to look at them, even less how to show them. Le Corbusier's insight is still alive; the eyes keep on not seeing and Kassovitz's eyes see no more than the others'. The old saying still stands: even with the best of intentions, hate is blind.

(Translated from the French by Anne-Sophie Cerisola)

1. Le Corbusier, *L'Esprit nouveau.*
2. *Mon Oncle.* The Arpel's modern house is the true hero of the movie. It is a manifestation of the triumphant fifties style, and, as such, it entered ordinary language. Now, every house from the fifties and the sixties, as long as it has some stylistic traits, is called a "house-of-mon-oncle."
3. The Ideal Home Exhibition.
4. The "Thirty Glorious Years" are the years between 1945 and 1973, during which France experienced an unprecedented growth in its economy and a modernization of its society.
5. *Beur* is a slang term for a French citizen born in France whose parents were born in once-French North Africa.

Yves Nacher is an architect, curator of the Institut français d'architecture, and president of the International Forum of Young Architects (IFYA), French section.

Françoise Zamour is a professor of film studies at the University of Lyon-II Auguste-et-Louis-Lumiere.

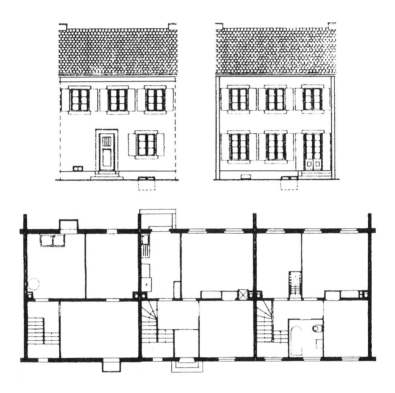

Facade and plan of a house constructed in 1920–21

The Territory Versus the City: Origins of an Anti-Urban Condition

Daniel Marco, with Giordano Tironi

The Power of the Country

At the end of the eighteenth century the Swiss, with the exception of a minority in some alpine cantons, lived in rural societies ruled by urban oligarchies. At the time, the country dominated demographically and economically, while the city had the political upper hand, which allowed for its economical exploitation of the country. In 1798, when revolutionary French soldiers entered Switzerland, their motto was "liberty, equality, fraternity," and their goal the liberation of all people oppressed by absolutism. For Switzerland, this meant the emancipation of the country from the city. In 1848, the winners of the civil war (or *Sonderbund*), still inspired by the French triptych, wrote the first federal constitution, which sanctified the Swiss antiurban culture. All power was transferred from the cities to the cantons, and the federal government controlled only the railways, the mail, the army, and foreign policy. For the Swiss, federalism was the political expression of the idea of liberty, while the old myth of an Alpine society—where peasants breathed pure air and lead a life of freedom and simplicity, and where all conflicts were solved by a democratic discussion—was the social expression of the ideas of equality and fraternity. This old Arcadian myth was reproduced at the 1896 International Exhibit of Geneva, where an enormous artificial Alpine landscape, forty meters high and peopled with imported mountain people, like a zoo, was built. The country physically occupied the city.

In turn-of-the-century Switzerland, the city was seen as the embodiment of an ideology of difference and inequality. This antiurban feeling grew stronger during the twenties and the thirties, as a reaction against forced industrialization, and again in the sixties. Moreover, the antiurban attitude was enhanced by unnecessariness for the emergence of a metropolis—or, as the *Littré Dictionary* defines it, "the mother of all cities." Because factories used dams and hydroelectric factories as their main energy supply, industrial production was decentralized until at least World War I. This decentralization allowed the numerous peasants who had become workers to stay at home, in their farms, thus creating some important consequences. As opposed to residents of the city, for whom social order was provided by the police, villagers in the country provided for their own order.

Only in the second half of the nineteenth century did economic and demographic concentration, made possible by the development of railways and electricity, begin. However, the political power of the country was further legitimized during the same period by the development of an important peasant lobby that fought for and ultimately won numerous economic incentives. The peasant lobby is still powerful today. According to the historian William Rappard, the homogeneity of the "rural class" explains its ability to fight victoriously against urban enemies who are much less united. "How many common problems do small and big retailers, artisans, entrepreneurs, workers, civil servants, and doctors have in common?"[1]

The Cooperative Movement

The Swiss antiurban ideology found its ideal expression in the cooperative movement of the interwar years. The cooperative movement has a strong political, social, and cultural influence in Switzerland. It was born from the unions and, since its beginnings in the nineteenth century, had a particular impact on workers' leisure time; it organized reading and writing classes, conferences, and excursions. Founded in 1843, the Société Suisse du Grutil—a popular cultural association, according to its statutes—was one of the most important of the associations that sought to organize the activities of the working class.

During the interwar years, the cooperative movement developed considerably, and extended its activities to housing, forming cooperative housing societies. Through their leaders, usually former unionized workers, these societies sought to intervene on the real-estate market, and proposed some very specific housing models—the garden city and the living colony. These models developed more rapidly in German-speaking Switzerland than in the French-speaking one. The most significant of the garden cities were Neubuhl in Zurich, built in 1930–31, and Freidorf in Basel, built in 1919–21.[2] In these cities, all the dwellings were only two stories high, and the windows opened onto a vegetable garden. According to the historian Jacques Gubier,

> [Freidorf] is a direct reference to [Jean-Jacques] Rousseau: the garden city is the opportunity "to go back to nature," to be liberated from the urban and industrial slavery, offered to the members of the cooperative. The entire operation is presented as a flight to the country.... The community guarantees the domestic tranquillity of its members. Each family can express its personality through the fantasy of the horticultural detail or a garden particularly well-kept.[3]

From the cooperative movement, the Left, the unions, and the political parties close to them inherited a vision of the city as a collection of dwellings. Indeed, a dwelling is concrete, good, isolable, exchangeable, quantifiable, and suitable for an interventionist economy. On the contrary, the city is an immaterial reality, where too interventionist an action can be dangerous. As a result, the birth of real urban planning in Switzerland still lied in the future.

Concentrated Decentralization

Since the forties, Switzerland has known a type of planning that could be defined as "concentrated decentralization." This concept was introduced in 1949 by Hans Carol and Marx Werner in their *Städte wie wir sie wünschen* (Towns Like We Want Them), a book that was the result of a four-year study of an interdisciplinary group named the Workshop for National Planning.[4] In the book, Carol and Werner appealed to the Swiss authorities and policy makers. The book's main thesis was not new; it was an expansion of Armin Meili's ideas on the dangers of urbanization that he had presented in his 1932 project, "Frogen der Landesplaung—Landesplaung für die Schweiz" (A Largely Decentralized Big Swiss City).[5] Carol and Werner also referred to Hans Bernhard, who, in 1919, produced a theory on industrial agriculture and internal colonization, as well as to the numerous architects, such as Hans Bernouilli, Camille Martin, and Henri-Robert von der Muhl, who used this theory in national planning projects based on the creation and development of colonies.

Since 1949, concentrated decentralization has been constantly used, in particular in the Master Plan CK-73 of 1973,[6] and in a report from the Federal Council on Planning of 1987. Indeed, as the historian André Corboz noted, "the concept of national planning was added to the Constitution only in 1969, and it took ten more years to pass a law; after that, the cantons relented, they had no intention of implementing the law, even though urbanization was unchecked."[7] Finally, the Federal Council published the Report on the Main Lines of Planning that concluded a large consultation led during 1995 by the Federal Bureau of Planning. In the report, the same ideas expressed by Carol and Werner can be found, in particular the notion that the territory is like a puzzle to be reconstructed. As usual, this old idea was used at a time when a crisis shook the foundations of the "House of Switzerland." Only then was everyone reminded of the equality between cantons, of the federal solidarity at local and national levels, of the beauty of the landscape of lakes, rivers, and mountains, and, on the other hand, of the threat of concrete that can eat up the country, of the anarchical growth of cities, and of unchecked tourism that ruins natural sites.

Armin Meili, the pioneer of Swiss planning, gave the best definition of concentrated decentralization. His goal was to control the growth of the big city by preventing a "gloved finger" form of development, which is a radial development along communication networks between cities. Instead, he proposed the creation of a network of living colonies of 10,000 inhabitants at the most, from Geneva to Saint-Gall, that would form a linear metropolis of six million people. The colonies would be linked to each other by public transportation. With this type of development, each person would benefit from the best of city life (education, libraries, museums, theaters) while staying in permanent contact with nature.

The idea of a pendulous movement between city and country had been best formulated by Rousseau, who was born in Switzerland. The writings of this famous philosopher shed light on why the Swiss produced such an antiurban culture, where each urban project is in fact a defense of the country in disguise. But, after all, who would ever have expected to find a mill in a ravine? In the whole world, only Switzerland presents this mixture of wild nature and human industry. The whole of Switzerland is, so to speak, only a large city whose streets, wider and longer than the Rue St. Antoine, are sown with forests, cut by mountains, and whose sparse and isolated houses have only English gardens as a link between them.[6]

(Translated from the French by Anne-Sophie Cerisola)

1. William Rappard, *Villes et campagnes swisses: leur évolution politique et économique depuis le fin de l'ancien régime a jusqué à nos jours* (Genava: Eggimann Editeur, 1916), 33.
2. Freidorf means "free village" in German.
3. Jacques Gubler, *Nationalisme et Internationalisme dans l'architecture moderne de la Suisse* (Lausanne: Editions L'Age d'homme, 1975).
4. Hans Carol and Max Werner, *Städte wie sie wir wünschen* (Zurich, 1949).
5. Armin Meili, "Frogen der Landesplaung—Landesplaung für die Schweiz" *Die Neue Stadt* 6/7 (1932): 142.
6. Département fédéral de Justice et Police, Conception directrice de l'aménagement du territoire CK-73 (Bern, 1973).
7. André Corboz, "Dans le vif de l'objet," introduction to F. Walter, *La Suisse Urbaine, 1750–1950* (Geneva, 1994).
8. Jean-Jacques Rousseau, *The Reveries of the Solitary Walker*, trans. and ed. by Charles Butterworth (Indianapolis: Hackett Publishing Company, 1992).

Daniel Marco is an architect and professor at the Architecture Institute at the University of Geneva. He is currently researching Swiss cities and studying housing rehabilitation, supported by the Swiss federal government.

Giordano Tironi is an architect practicing is Switzerland, Italy, and France. He is a profesor at the School of Architecture at Grenoble, and has worked on industrial -scale projects and landscapes.

New Towns
Graham Carnaffan

A tight knot balls up in my stomach as I drive north and home.
As the land rises slowly, tilting towards the Scottish border, the
green slowly develops into a swathe of gray, undulating across
the floor of the Tyne Valley until it conglomerates into one concrete mass. This mass is commonly known as Washington.
Washington, Tyne and Wear, England. Its origins stretch back
to the eighteenth century, when coal ruled the vast industrial
Tyne Valley. Washington was then a small village of solid stone
housing built from the local quarries, surrounded by ever damp
and flat pasture lands. George Washington's ancestors had their
roots here. The best thing they ever did was to leave, to get out
when the going was good and produce a famous son elsewhere.

As the eighteenth and nineteenth centuries passed, Washington sat content as a village while all around industrialization
changed the landscape of the surrounding towns. Fifteen miles
to the north lies the city of Newcastle upon Tyne. From this
riverside city, coal, steel, and ships were spewed out *en masse*,
and with them came the crammed housing synonymous with
heavily industrialized areas. "Back to backs" we call them—the
once proud red brick terraced houses where the women could be
seen on their knees scrubbing the front stoop. By the end of the
Second World War, Newcastle was bursting at the seams and
diseases such as tuberculosis ran rampant in the crammed
spaces that had become some of the worst slums in the United

Kingdom. The stigma of poverty is all too prevalent there. Even today, opposing football fans visiting Newcastle still chant, "In your Newcastle slums, you look in the dustbin for something to eat, you find a dead rat and you think it's a treat, in your Newcastle slums."

Aye, coals from Newcastle. Lying low in the embers and scratched out of the potato and wheat fields, the village of Washington slept under the ever-expanding shadow of Newcastle. Clearly, the need for decent and affordable housing had reached a crisis point by the end of the Second World War. Washington was earmarked for development. The first thing to come was all these damned roads. The main north-south route at that time was the Great North Road, commonly called the A-I. Following the same path that the Romans laid centuries ago, it stretches from London to Edinburgh, cutting a path through Newcastle, and bypassing Washington. Extra lanes were added and the old road was transformed into a modern, efficient motorway—the M-I. Washington became encircled within a loop, spliced apart with slip roads and byways, overpasses and passing lanes. I drive straight as an arrow. It is so easy to get lost around here.

Town limits were set by the loop. Washington Newtown was promoted as a clean, orderly place to live and raise a family. The town planners had copied their American counterparts in the design and conception of Washington Newtown. Each neighborhood was subdivided with yet more roads and then numbered. Each unit of housing came with a small garden, a driveway for the car, and a neighborhood that was identical to the adjoining one. These neighborhoods were named district one, two, three, etc., and all were accessible from a slew of motorway exits. The concept of an urban utopia lay within grasp, except for the fact that car ownership was a rarity in the sixties and seventies (only one in three families owned a car).

In an effort to promote social unity and identification, the state had looked toward socialism for inspiration. The demand of Newcastle residents to be relocated was huge. The population's sense of aesthetics had been blunted by the stench of heavy industry, so the fact that the new town resembled a series of concrete rabbit hutches did not dismay them. Washington Newtown was clean and had all the amenities of urban life concentrated within the confines of the new circular roads that were laid. The myriad roads and concrete divided and isolated the community, and public transportation found it increasingly difficult to create a hub amid the sprawl.

Then came the recession of the early seventies, along with devastating cutbacks in local government spending. Washington Newtown was finished with cheap materials, such as "clapboard," a factory-finished, fabricated siding. Now, the locals outside the loop refer to Washington Newtown as "cardboard city." The rot had set in before the project was finished.

Today the prospects of employment hurtle south along the motorway. In certain areas of Washington Newtown, the unemployment rate hovers around thirty percent. The local government has employed a few thousand youths to cut grass, clean windows, and sweep roads in an attempt to lend character to perhaps one of the dullest housing experiments in the United Kingdom.

I arrive to see concrete bunkers projecting into the gray sky as the whoop of a police siren pierces the bleakness. A mirage of radioactive red mingles with a seductive blue. The regular army of underfed skinheads is lurking around the corner shop that sells loose cigarettes and strong cider, sniffing glue. It stinks of boredom and shit around here. Trodden upon and left with an indelible shoe print, these small piles of organic matter offer proof of life. Then of course there are the bloody dogs that roam around, sniffing, shitting, and breeding conspicuously. These vagabonds snarl at each other and fight over the ever-decreasing open spaces.

That brings me to the conclusion that pretty damned soon this whole town will be paved and smoothed over in the eternal conquest for suburban euthanasia. We have come to a dead end in this town of new towns. The dream of congregating in one isolated place, as the motorways and slip roads bypass and encircle, drives one to believe that we are all entrapped in some encampment. This place where the people have been relocated and divided seems not unlike an Indian reservation on the fifty-fifth parallel, twenty miles from nowhere and closer to oblivion than we think.

Graham Carnaffan was born and raised in the industrial city of Newcastle Upon Tyne and has lived in New York for the last four years. He is currently working on a collection of short stories and is translating his poetry into the Gaelic language.

Stalker

Lorenzo Romito

Rome, a city with 3.5 million inhabitants, is the largest agricultural commune of Europe. It combines dimensions of a metropolitan scale and a high-flux density together with vast open spaces, where one can encounter sheep grazing in fields crossed by ancient aqueducts, modern transmission towers, and nomad camps. The city encompasses different conceptions of space and time due to the nature of its complex orography and historical evolution. In the city's over-two-thousand-year history, it has first expanded and then contracted at various times—from over a million inhabitants in Imperial Rome, to less than a few thousand during the Middle Ages—to become today a modern metropolis.

Throughout this pulsating process, the city has generated vast abandoned areas. Though extremely rich in history and fertile ground for the future, they lack an important present dimension. These "vague terrains," today a topical issue, have always been a peculiarity of this city. Similar spaces exist today in all major modern cites, to such an extent that they have been typologically individualized, but not everywhere have they reached such a morphological richness and such an extensive and complicated presence as they have in the city of Rome. I believe these areas offer the most insight into the great complexity of the nature of the city and the evolution of the modern metropolis.

View toward Balduina

The laboratory for territorial researches—Stalker—explored these interstitial spaces of the city of Rome from 5–9 October 1995, the first journey through what we call "actual territories," empty spaces that are abandoned or in transformation. We covered about forty-three miles on foot without ever leaving the city, but without ever entering it properly either, through areas that are unknown and invisible to most, though they cover a vast territorial extension, maybe larger than the built city itself.

We started our journey with the aim of returning to the starting point, the unused train station of Vigna Clara, after having crossed the entire city on self-created tracks that had never before been made. Our traveling took us across fences, railroad tracks, and highways, linking places that are now permanently disconnected; it also allowed us to discover new and huge distances between contiguous neighborhoods. We spent hours to cover areas that are connected in minutes by car. We traveled on the city's negative side to witness its existence, to perceive its autonomous evolution distant from its actual site, and therefore distant from the control of humans. We undertook this route especially to demonstrate the rich articulation, the continuity, and the deep penetration of these areas around the entire city.

Our anxiety in entering spaces that lack a main door, tearing apart wire netting, and climbing over walls made our senses continuously alert, our movements cautious; territorial cognition became linked with survival, restoring to our sight the capacity of observation. Through this experience we crossed a territory, and its discovery became a creative statement. We realized a continuous but at the same time tortuous and unexpected path that transformed the chaotic and casual relations that occur between nature and the discarded human waste, that, combining themselves in a process of mutual transformation, distinguish these spaces.

We traveled through the past and the future of the city, through its lost memories and its unconscious becoming, in a territory created by mankind, beyond his will. In this void we designed an ephemeral subjective geography, instantaneous statements of a world in constant transformation. In fact, we created a space without having planned or built it, by simply

crossing it. This makes our experience an "architectural practice." We believe

the space that belongs to architecture is not a geometrical
and individualized place, it is not an ideal projection of
human thought or *container* of our *being-in-the-world*, but in
daily reality, it is our same *being-in-the-world* that is invisible
and undistinguished.[1]

Today more and more architects work on the marginal grounds
of the discipline, using behavior that does not escape from architecture, but expresses the desire to contaminate architecture
itself. This contamination evolves through the creation of new
and paradigmatic "containers" of architecture, through the realization of a path, an existentialist practice, that consents to
mature the consciousness of the world's becoming and of our
taking part in evolution.

Plan behaviors instead of formal volumetrics, either when
imposed by political power or when inherited from custom
or from the modern tradition. One must tend to a society
without a father, one must be able to desume spatial qualities and behaviors from the right of autodetermination, that
does not consent to delegate under any form. To aim for the
compelling need to verify scientifically proven conjectures
on space, to be able to combine the revolution of architecture
to the struggle for the transformation of political structures.
In conclusion, the goal is the creation of a passage from a
formalistic idea of space to the reality of the daily experienced space.[2]

The world, through modern technologies, is evolving into a
global village in which huge distances have disappeared because
of the growing speed of the connective network. Through the
fractures and the separations generated by those same systems,
the city has become an environment where one can encounter
new spaces and insurmountable distances. The voids in the
urban context, in a similar fashion as in oceans, are crossed by
rapid connecting ways, beneath which deep and unexplored
worlds are hidden.

The press coverage of our journey was quite unexpected,
considering the fact that it was an elusive operation, marginal
and difficult to define. The first article was published on the day

we started out in a left-wing, slightly intellectual newspaper, which contacted us on our return for a second article. Since then we have been contacted by anthropologists, philosophers, sociologists, art critics, and even by a fashion magazine and a television production. Finally, an architectural magazine, that was not Italian but French, published an article about us.

We started to travel through a different archipelago, made not out of built-up islands, but formed by isolated worlds, where different disciplines configure themselves autonomously through their own communication systems. This immaterial world bears the same characteristics of the global village, where huge communication highways tend to make the relations between these islands homogeneous and bland, although they still maintain their qualities of self-reference and of reciprocal indifference. Here we found more and more, vast and deep voids, territories able to contain huge distances, new and infinite spaces that are meant to be crossed without a precise aim, but with a nomadic and observing attitude that John Keats called "negative capacity," in which "a man is capable of being in uncertainties, mysteries, doubts, without any irritable reaching after fact and reason."[3]

Friday 6 October 1995

We left at 11:00 yesterday morning from the Vigna Clara Station, but only today have I reached that minimum of tranquillity necessary to compose a travel diary.

It was nine in the morning and we woke up in a small soccer field; it must be the work of a community of Albanians who live nearby in a couple abandoned buildings.

Andrea, our "Sherpa," should have showed up by now, with his little red Fiat wagon, the "red flower," to take out our tents and sleeping bags. Before he arrives I will try to list a couple things that happened yesterday.

The departure from Vigna Clara held no surprises, and there was a lot of satisfaction over the photo article published in La Republica[4] even if the contents of the article, not to mention the photo (children in a nomad camp), were highly inaccurate with respect to the operation we had planned to undertake. We were, however, enthusiastic that there appeared together in block capital letters the words "ART" and "NOMADS."

Having left the station the ten of us followed a section of the incomplete ring of the railroad, counting on meeting Gregorio with his sheep. The shepherd was not there; maybe he had begun his urban transmigration most likely towards Roma-Sud, the south of Rome.

We arrived at the bank of the Tiber and called to Alfredo the fisherman with a whistle. He appeared immediately with a motorboat, and he asked us to wait a half hour while he got out his flat-bottomed boat to ferry us across to the opposite bank. He got back much sooner, and with extreme ease we crossed the river.

We followed along the curving flood banks of the Aniene. Between the river and the bank, where the compact part of the city faces, there were a little less than ten meters of thick cane growth cut by a trail marked with larger clearings, framed by vaults of cane, inhabited here and there by a tent or a barrack. We only encountered one small family. We said hello, then asked them for directions that we did not follow, since we continued where they told us it was impossible to pass.

Piccio went on ahead of us. We found him some ways further up spreading flour on twelve large cylinders of cement that we would eventually have to cross. When everyone in the group caught up, Piccio opened a bottle of wine and poured it out over the whole row of flour-covered cylinders. Having celebrated this "gate," we passed through it, trying to draw energy from the sanctity of the act just completed. Someone did not miss the chance to express less than mythic impressions on the quality of the wine.

We encountered several bath tubs, which we rattled violently to make them sound like drums.

Up ahead a few dogs blocked our road; we succeeded in passing anyway, but not without a good fright. We arrived at a drainage bridge, which we intended to climb to get across the river Aniene. The operation was not very easy, as we had to hoist ourselves up with a rope. Once on the other side, we faced new complications; we found ourselves five meters above ground level and did not know how to get down. We asked for help, and from a nearby shack a man came out with a ladder to help us down.

Tromba suveying abandoned railroad *Art of nomads*

Crossing the Tiber on Alfredo's boat

"Flower and Wine on Concrete Cylinders," installation by Piccio

A reflection on waste

Unfinished business

LORENZO ROMITO

Now Andrea has arrived, and it is time to leave for the day's walk. One last thing. Yesterday we arrived an hour late for our scheduled meeting with Andrea at six, and it was almost all dark. We had just enough time to enjoy the spectacle of all those huge blue and yellow cylinders that serve as air vents and elevator towers for the Quintiliani Metro Station. They stick out from nowhere in the middle of a green valley and create a sound that is rhythmically timed to the passage of the fast trains below.

We take off again.

Saturday, 7 October 1995
Second wake-up call. We are on a plane of volcanic tuff, this place is like Monument Valley. We had set up our tents in the saddle of three small hills. A number of ancient caves are here, and we are only a few paces away from the Fosse Ardeatide and the San Callisto Catacombs.

Last night we cooked a huge barbecue with some guests, some of whom remained. Now the group is a bit larger. Marco (Giovanna's husband) arrived, Guido (a geologist), and Silvana. They joined our committee originally composed of Aldo "Tromba," Giovanna, Massimo Martini (who considers himself too old to camp the nights with us), Francesco "Piccio," Paolo "Pinnochio," Romolo, my brother Valerio, and yours truly, Lorenzo. Last night at dinner we also had over Carlotta, Caroline, and Ilaria. This morning Ilaria came back to join us, and Andrea left his Fiat and is coming with us.

Andrea has suggested that we reflect on the word "waste" (*scarto*). For him, it is a question of being outmoded; Tromba, who was also in on the conversation, thinks that regardless of whether an object still has use, it is just garbage. I would like to give more space to an epistemological research on the word "waste," but I have another issue in mind, and very little time to write notes before we start up again.

Last night we slept at the place where ancient Christians once gathered to celebrate, in secret, their own rituals. This place has always remained outside Rome's official history. We have to go.

Sunday, 8 October 1995
Wake up call at 7:30 in an unfinished six-lane highway with numerous new overpasses. We call it the "dromodromo," a space that is perfectly adapted to holding camel races, due to its compressed sand roadway.

The viaduct that crosses the valley where we are camping is strangely peculiar. Nothing goes by on it other than tourist buses. In one direction the buses go by empty, and in the other they are filled with tourists. We attentively studied the question. Our first hypothesis was that these tourists already know we intend to hold camel races here, a hypothesis immediately rejected. After a bit more reflection we hazard a theory that is more plausible. Given the importance of the tourist industry in light of the upcoming millennium jubilee, it is possible that right here on the Portuense is a factory that anticipated the production of those twenty million tourists that everyone talks about and that are expected in Rome in 2000.

In the meantime yet another bus filled with tourists has gone by and we photographed them. Through the smoked glass windows of the Pullman we were able to capture their expressions of stupefaction. They saw us; some with paternalistic pity waved hello. Out of decency almost no one photographed us. But when we turned our photo and video cameras on them, we read in their faces a crisis of identity—a group of German tourists photographed, crossing over a viaduct, by some nomads camped below. There is a good chance that some of them will be experiencing shock for some time to come.

What happened yesterday?

We started by crossing a marvelous valley cultivated primarily with rosemary and sage, an almost uncontaminated place, where the only sign of mutation in process were five huge cranes dismantled and heaped across the fields.

After this valley we reached EUR[5] and we went through an amusement park. Then we continued on past the Hippodrome and the nomad camps of Tor di Valle. We had to pass burning fields to reach the banks of the Tiber. We crossed the Tiber using an aqueduct bridge built by the ACEA water authority. Not everyone was with us; a smaller group, consisting of Tromba, Pinnochio, and Piccio, were moving autonomously.

We climbed up the small hill dominated by the ruins of the "Trullo," from where one could enjoy a magnificent view of EUR. We reached our evening rendezvous tremendously tired and behind schedule. What really did us in was finding a dozen friends waiting for us to see who knows what. We had early organizational difficulties, and we made a poor choice with this camp site. No one had brought anything to eat, and so everyone disappeared.

So we installed ourselves in this magnificent place where now Guido, the geologist, is playing his clarinet. The sound penetrates into the openings of the sewage canals just built.

Monday, 9 October 1995

Its 10:30, I am home, I just woke up, the voyage is over.

The last encounter that we had was perhaps the most unexpected: a porcupine, right in the middle of an underground gallery over four kilometers long. In the film *Stalker* by Andrei Tarkovskii (the title inspired our initiative), the nickname of the first mythical guide across the mutant zone is Porcupine. Maybe this was a simple error in the translation. Maybe that porcupine that we encounter this night was none other than Porcupine coming to say hello. One is more likely to find a stalker at the bottom of a tunnel than a porcupine.

This night, coming out of the tunnel, we put our feet back right where we started out four days ago at the inauguration of crossing actual territories. We got out of our journey imprecise descriptions. All we did was walk, be in places, cross them, and tie their destiny to ours. Every time we climbed over a wall or we went through a hole in a chain-link fence, we experienced apprehension, which made us more attentive to these unknown places, even if they are in our backyard.

These existing terrains have been unveiled. We have the key to their access; we know where to return to listen to the voice, to sing the streets, to celebrate the locations, but also to conduct any others who might feel the need to discover.

(Translated from the Italian by Livia Tani)

1. Cesare Brandi, "La spazialità antiprospettica," in Bruno Zevi, ed., *Architettura concetti di una controstoria* (Rome: Newton Compton, 1994), 74.
2. Aldo Loris Rossi and D. Mazzoleni, "Spazio e comportamento," in Zevi, *Architettura concetti*, 72.
3. John Keats, cited in Richard Sennett, *The Conscience of the Eye* (New York: W W Norton, 1990), 248.
4. *La Republica* is the second largest national daily in Italy, after the *Corriere della Sera*.
5. Esposizione Universale di Roma, a modern neighborhood in the south of Rome built by Benito Mussolini in the 1940s to host a universal exposition. Its architecture is highly evocative of the period.

The original members of Stalker are Paolo "Pinocchio" Bruschi, Francesco "Piccio" Careri, Aldo "Tromba" Innocenzi, Guido Lanci, Giovanna Ripepi, Romolo Ottaviani, Lorenzo Romito, and Valerio Romito. Stalker is currently involved in mapping Rome and its periphery and is also working in the city regions of Milan, Naples, Turin, Berlin, Orleans, and Paris.

StoreFront for Art and Architecture
is a not-for-profit organization established in 1982. StoreFront's programs are supported by: The Andy Warhol Foundation for the Visual Arts, Inc., The Greenwall Foundation, The Jerome Foundation, The J. M. Kaplan Fund, The Graham Foundation for Advanced Studies in the Fine Arts, The LEF Foundation, The Joyce Mertz Gilmore Foundation, The Reed Foundation, The Rockefeller Foundation, The National Endowment for the Arts, The New York State Council on the Arts, The New York City Department of Cultural Affairs, and individual contributors.

StoreFront Books
is dedicated to the exploration and mapping of new world disorder and its architecture. A continuation and expansion of our previous publications, *Reports* and *Front*, this series will provide documentation and commentary relating to StoreFront exhibitions and other programs. StoreFront Books reflects a cultural mosaic of issues concerning the environment, technology, ecology, and aesthetics. Along with upcoming volumes, *Suburban Discipline* presents StoreFront for Art and Architecture as a living proof of cultural resistance.

StoreFront for Art and Architecture
97 Kenmare Street, New York, NY 10012
tel. 212.431.5795   fax 212.431.5755